CONUNDRA

Pat + Lawrence,
Thank you for your support.
Gerald

Gerald M. Sliva

CONUNDRA

The Golden Rule Revisited

A quest for the meaning of life

Gerald M. Sliva

Gerald M. Sliva

Dedication

This book is dedicated to the love of my life, Cecilia, my wife of 55 years; our son, Greg; our daughter-in-law, Grace; and our granddaughter, Robyn. You are precious to me.

Copyright © 2019 Gerald M. Sliva
All rights reserved
ISBN-978170582194
No part of this book may be reproduced in any manner except by the express permission of the author who may be contacted at **myconundra@gmail.com**

Cover image by Gerd Altmann from Pixabay

Table of Contents

Dedication	iv
Prologue	1
Chapter 1 Revealing the Secret	4
Chapter 2 Old Clothes Feel Good	7
Part 1 – Youth	12
Chapter 3 Born a Muslim	13
Chapter 4 Faith of Our Fathers	16
Chapter 5 Український католик (Ukrainian Catholic)	27
Chapter 6 Erotic Encounters	36
Chapter 7 Political Naivety	41
Chapter 8 Political Suicide	45
Part 2 – Exploration	49
Chapter 9 Accident or Design	50
Chapter 10 Man, the Manipulator	57
Chapter 11 Mis-Understanding the Bible	62
Chapter 12 Space Invaders	71

Part 3 – Faith and Fraud	76
Chapter 13 True Belief – Faith	77
Chapter 14 Common Ground	81
Chapter 15 Finding Jesus	84
Chapter 16 Church, Faith, Fraud	95
Part 4 – Religious Politi-Sex	101
Chapter 17 Bathroom Debacle	102
Chapter 18 Celibacy, a Catholic Conundrum	108
Part 5 – Prayer	117
Chapter 19 Thy Kingdom Come	118
Chapter 20 Prayers of Charity	122
Chapter 21 Talking With Jesus	129
Chapter 22 Talking with God	131
Chapter 23 Prayerful Tears	136
Chapter 24 Mystical Messages	141
Part 6 – After Life	150
Chapter 25 Eternal Cosmic Suits	151
Chapter 26 Our Bodies are Caterpillars; Our Souls, Butterflies	154
Chapter 27 Making Heaven/Creating Hell	163
Chapter 28 Packing My Bags	166
Epilogue	170

Meditation, Reflection, Discussion 172

Acknowledgements 185

Bibliography, Reference and Reading List 188

"Walk with those seeking truth...
run from those who think they've found it."

- DEEPAK CHOPRA

Prologue

"The trilogy composed of politics, religion and sex is the most sensitive of all issues in any society" - *Nawal El Saadawi*

This book is primarily about religion. The good, the bad and the ugly, and sometimes also the beautiful! But it also veers into politics and sex.

Conundra is a non-standard pluralisation of "conundrum". I chose "Conundra" as my book title to reflect the contradictions, confusion and some hypocrisy regarding stated religious and political beliefs juxtaposed with observable actions.

One unknown person's sage advice: "Common etiquette says not to talk about politics, sex, religion, or money. But these are the most interesting things to discuss!" Another learned man (Charles M. Schulz, creator of the *Peanuts* comic strip) said, "There are three things I have learned never to discuss with people ... religion, politics and the Great Pumpkin!" Considering the wisdom of these two advisors, I have resolutely determined to avoid discussions of money or The Great Pumpkin. The other three topics are fair game: religion, sex and politics.

There is little that makes me more uncomfortable than someone shoving religion or politics down my throat. I assume that I am not far from the norm. So, I will try not to preach. Asking questions rather than providing answers, I will deliberately explore my own religious beliefs (as well as sexual and political ones where they seem to intersect with religion). Beginning with my childhood experiences, I take the reader on an essay journey of inquiry, investigation and discovery. The book is structured so that each chapter may be read somewhat independently; yet each is linked by the common theme of *The Golden Rule* and its relevance to everyday life.

I am examining my own beliefs and faith or lack thereof; by reading the words written herein, I hope the reader may do the same: *consider, examine and think*. Perhaps, think critically about issues more important than standing in line for the newest iPhone, learning what the Kardashians are doing, shopping for the latest fashions, watching the trendiest reality show, deciding what clothes to wear, or which hairstyle is in vogue. The quotations at the beginning of, and within each chapter are not intended to be taken as truths. They are intended to generate thoughts, and maybe even actions.

More than ever, with ongoing regional conflicts, global refugee and migrant crises, political upheaval and the trending disillusionment with traditional religions, I see a need to critically examine a variety of aspects of religion and spirituality together with man's relationship to man as well as man's relationship to his God.

But I also want to have some fun. Seems to me one can only be serious for so long about religion, sex or politics without going mad. That calls for a lighthearted approach, but also for some earnest soul-searching. Can I lend humour to religion without being irreverent, wit to politics without being partisan, and levity, or even buffoonery to sex without being vulgar? Thank you for joining me. We will open our minds to explore Religious Politi-Sex together. My hope is to inspire, inform, entertain and inquire. As we begin, perhaps a statement attributed to George H. W. Bush would set the mood: "I have opinions of my own - strong opinions – but I don't always agree with them."

Chapter 1
Revealing the Secret

"This is what happens. You tell your friends your most personal secrets, and they use them against you." - Sophie Kinsella, "Shopaholic Ties the Knot"

Do you find it unusual, even bizarre, that someone with no theological education, no background in political science and no training as a sex therapist would attempt to write about religion, sex and politics? Can I trust you with the secret of the real reason I am writing this book? I've never told anyone this secret, not my wife, not my son, not my closest friends. No one! Will you laugh, deride or mock me? Will I be the brunt of crude jokes? Will you think I'm nuts?

I'm writing this book because Jesus told me to.

There! I said it. I'm doing my part. I'm writing the book, as I've been commanded. The rest is up to you. I know that many of you will be convinced that I've lost my marbles, gone off the deep end. Jesus told me that would be the reaction of most of my family, my closest friends and my readers. Will it be used against me?

Conundra

You must find it hard to believe that anyone would get a personal message from Jesus. If someone told *me* this story, I would be incredulous too. In fact, I would probably doubt the person's sanity. My reaction would be to change the subject or make a quick exit. Many people try to connect with Jesus through prayer, but when someone tells me that Jesus gives them personal messages and specific instructions, I'm thinking they've got to have a few screws loose. So, I have to tell you about how and when I met Jesus and what he really told me.

It started like this. Almost every day I visit the **cac.org** website where Richard Rohr posts his daily meditations. Some days, much as I try, I am unable to relate to his thoughts. But at other times - Tuesday October 30, 2018 was one of those days – his words found a place in my heart. After reading the meditation I sat in my recliner, considering what the words meant to me. A peace, calmness, and loving warmth enveloped me as I heard the voice of Jesus telling me to write a book about religion, sex and politics. He told me that it would turn me into a bestselling author. As a result of my book's popularity I would have the opportunity to spread the Good News by starting a new religion which would gather people from all parts of the globe into a loving relationship.

Who would believe me? Not many! But there would be some believers.

In fact, I really **did not** get a message from Jesus. But if I really wanted to embellish the story even more with Jesus' voice coming from the heavens, the clouds or a burning bush, I might get a few more believers, people willing to support a new religion, especially if I promised them untold wealth now and eternal salvation later. And if I were an especially charismatic speaker who held revivals and inspirational speaking tours, people might have blind faith and believe my bizarre story. Some might even give away their fortune because some smooth-talking con artist – that would be me - convinced them that Jesus told him to raise five million dollars to buy a jet plane so he could fly to the other side of the planet to convert the heathen hordes. There may be some people who either get direct messages from Jesus or God, or they imagine they do, but I certainly did not. Flimflam men and scammers abound. In the age of fake news on social media, salvation-touting con artists and rampant boldfaced lies by some politicians, is there a need for our educational systems to prioritize training in critical thinking?

    The real reason I am writing this book is described in the next chapter.

Chapter 2
Old Clothes Feel Good

"I wore my faith like the shirt I fell asleep in because I was too lazy to change." - Leanne Oelke, "Nice Try, Jane Sinner"

As I grew up, I was relatively certain I had faith, but perhaps it was fake faith. Was it like that wrinkled shirt that I was too lazy to change? Maybe I had work to do.

For years, after making notes and jotting down quotes on religion, relationships and spirituality, I knew I wanted to compile them into a book. Maybe I was too lazy, maybe uninspired, or perhaps uncertain of my direction. For a few years I had been reading and considering the daily meditations of Father Richard Rohr. Then in the summer of 2018, after reading *Perspective, The Golden Rule* by David Meakes, my desire became an obsession. In the first one hundred or so pages, David describes his religious upbringing and his admiration for his father who was a lay preacher. In spite of it all, David is agnostic. Dr. David Meakes, Doctor of Podiatric Medicine, is a 96-year-old Canadian with permanent residency in the United States. He is an author, thinker, philosopher, and an idealist, socialist, anti-war and anti-military humanist. In studying the writings of the priest and the agnostic humanist, I was struck by the synchronicity of their messages. Despite his agnosticism, David frequently quotes the New Testament and promotes the brotherhood of man as well as the *Golden Rule*: Do unto others as you would have them do unto you. In fact, Dr. Meakes strongly advocates that the *Golden Rule* be taught in all schools worldwide from the earliest grades, continuing through high school and advanced education. I was intrigued by the man and his ideas, contacted him by email and developed an email friendship (we now call ourselves soul brothers). After getting to know David better I referred him to Richard Rohr's meditations, commenting that I felt they often had similar messages. For many months, by almost daily email communications, we considered, debated and referred to the meditations, with David himself noting the similarity in their messages, sometimes saying he and Father Richard were like two peas in a pod. So much so that I have facetiously threatened to contact Pope Francis to nominate David as the first agnostic saint.

Then, during the winter of 2019, while vacationing in Arizona, my wife, Cecilia and I visited with David at his home where we found him to be hale and hearty even at the age of 96. Knowing that I am writing a book about religion, David wants to help. He is definitely not anti-religious, proving it on our several visits by inundating me with religious, spiritual and humanist reference material consisting of some thirty books and countless magazines and articles, all to help make my book a best seller. The topics are varied: Christianity, the Amish, Buddhism, the Bible, prayer, mysticism, faith, spirituality and books about and by great thinkers like Martin Luther King, Albert Schweitzer, Nelson Mandela, Mahatma Gandhi and Confucius. This man, asserting to be agnostic, possessed more religious reference material than is available in any ten combined so-called Christian homes. Considering Dr. Meakes' profession of agnosticism, I was spurred to critically research religion and examine my own faith. Maybe even change that creased and wrinkled shirt. Here goes!

From the mid-20th century and on into the 21st century it has been trendy for comedians, authors, scientists and philosophers to expound agnostic, atheistic and anti-religious bias. For many good people there is increasing popularity in changing religions, giving up on religion entirely or searching for the meaning of life in less traditional venues. Perhaps not without justification! Many Bible thumping clergy, preachers and evangelists have been figuratively and literally caught with their pants down. Even more seriously, history has shown Christian fanatics to be ruthless crusaders, perpetrators of the Inquisition and merciless witch burners. More recently, radical Islamist terrorists screaming "Allahu Akbar" (God is Great) have slaughtered in the name of God. Can any religion be trusted?

This is a book about religion, but the evolution of my research revealed that religion is often bound up in politics and sex. Throughout history, powerful religious and political figures have succumbed to sexual temptation. With his alleged sexual indiscretions, Donald J. Trump would not the first, nor will he be the last. But with the dawning of Donald Trump (whether one adores him or despises him), religion, politics and sex are fully intertwined. Mr. Trump has been discovered making hush money payments to a stripper and a porn star in what – according to a December 10, 2018 Washington Post article - he calls "a simple private transaction", while having a massive base of staunchly Christian evangelical supporters. Ergo - politics, religion and sex have become so integrated that it becomes increasingly difficult to discuss religion without inserting overtones of politics and sex.

These are sensitive issues and becoming more so by the day. In doing some research, I considered the number of times men think of sex each day. Then I delved into the number of times women think of sex each day. While I examined my own experiences, prejudices and opinions, I wondered, "How many times a day do people think about God, religion, the spiritual realm?" Have these topics become more polarizing, more divisive with the recent scandals of sexual abuse of children by some Catholic clergy? Then I wondered, "How many times a day do people think of politics?" With the advent of Donald Trump where one-half of Americans regard him as a raving lunatic and the other half regard him as their saviour, I suspect – rather, I know – that politics is on the minds of people even more than sex or religion. Not only in America, but around the world!

Because I am neither a theologian, political scientist nor a Doctor Ruth you may ask yourself what gives me the knowledge, authority or the *balls* to assume that I have anything of value to contribute to the topics in question. But this is a quest for meaning, examining the authenticity of what I believe. Even novices can search and wonder and speculate. Do I hang on to my beliefs because I am too lazy or too fearful to assess them critically? Do I have doubts? Maybe uncertainty is an aid to true exploration.

Gerald M. Sliva

Part 1 – Youth

When I was young
I knew all the right answers;
Now that I'm old
I don't even know the right questions.

Chapter 3
Born a Muslim

"I yam what I yam, and that's all what I yam." - Popeye the Sailor Man

I yam what I yam for a variety of reasons: partially because of my religious upbringing, my educational experiences, the influences of my parents and siblings, as well as the pastoral environment of the small town in which I was raised. I was not born a Muslim, so "that's not what I yam". But it started me thinking about the circumstances of my birth and upbringing as well as that of every other person on this planet.

Not many weeks ago I read the heart-warming, humorous, and thought-provoking book, *Born a Crime* by Trevor Noah. The premise of his book title is that because he was the offspring of a white father and a black mother during apartheid, according to the laws in South Africa at the time, his birth was a criminal action. What if, instead of his birth being a crime, it was determined that the laws were a crime? What if many of our current laws, mostly laws made by the rich, the powerful, and the elite to preserve their wealth, status and power, are really the greater crime?

In some ways, is every birth, though not a crime, an accident of fate? I wondered what my life and my beliefs would they be like if I had been born in India, Africa, Poland, the USSR, Mexico or on a First Nations Reservation in Canada. What if I were black or brown, or yellow-skinned? What if I were female rather than male or what if gay or transsexual? What if severely mentally or physically disabled? What if my parents had been racists, murderers or thieves, physically, sexually or emotionally abusive and they had raised me to be the same? What if my parents had been Jewish, or Nazi, or Muslim, Buddhist, or atheist rather than Catholic Christian? What if I had never heard of God? Is there enough wonder in nature to motivate me to worship? What would my relationship be with strangers, my neighbours and my Creator in each of those circumstances? Would I be loved any more or any less?

If, rather than learning love, hospitality, respect and faith from my elders or peers, I was learning thievery, selfishness, racism, and cynicism, what would be my fate? Take thievery, for instance. I have no need to steal. I am blessed with all I need and more. Others, raised in abject poverty and without the opportunity for a good education or reasonable employment at a living wage, may have a necessity to steal to stay alive. It is their occupation, their career, their vocation from generation to generation, the children learning from the parents. Unless charitable folk or a benevolent government provide them with opportunity and sustenance, their lives depend on theft. Those of us who have no need to steal believe thievery to be immoral, a crime, and a sin. "Thou shalt not steal" is a clear commandment. Is it possible that perhaps, in some instances, thievery is not immoral, a sin or a crime? Instead, could the crime be the laws which favour the rich and powerful, encouraging greed, fear, selfishness and cynicism which indirectly force people into a life of theft for their very survival? What about prostitution, lying, cheating as well as theft? Does the necessity for survival override the Ten Commandments?

Are politicians and legislators criminals when they pass laws which favour the rich or themselves and their families? By doing so, do they directly or indirectly prevent certain parts of society from extricating themselves from the grips of poverty? Are religious leaders and lay people implicated?

Am I so prideful, smug and self-righteous as to believe that I am better than any other human being because of the accident of my birth? Am I so depressed, remorseful and pessimistic as to believe I am worse than any other human being because of the circumstances of my birth?

Chapter 4
Faith of Our Fathers

"My religious upbringing was comically strict — even the Dirt Devil vacuum cleaner was banned. In our house, no one was allowed to refer to devilled eggs. We had to call them angelic eggs. We were never allowed to swear. I'd get into trouble just for saying, 'Hell no'. If you dropped a hammer on your toe in our house you had to say something like 'Jiminy Christmas'. The only music we were allowed to listen to was gospel. No wonder I rebelled." - Katy Perry

We all have a starting point, a place from whence we begin the formation of our ideas, opinions, likes, dislikes, prejudices and attitudes. It starts with our family, developing and expanding from there. Our churches, relatives, peers, teachers, community and politicians, even our local, regional and national governments contribute to the mosaic of our lives. This is true of our mental images of God, church and religion.

Almost all of us are raised in the faith traditions of our parents, whether Christian, Jewish, Hindu, Sikh, Muslim, atheist or agnostic. In our youth, we just accepted that our upbringing was the best. Most of us never questioned, researched or investigated alternatives. We were certainly not encouraged to think (Maybe our Creator wouldn't like us to think.) about whether our beliefs made sense.

I was raised as a Roman Catholic. It seems to me, as well as to several of my peers, that in the middle of the twentieth century, Catholicism was more than a religion. It was a way of life. In small town Saskatchewan, as in most villages and towns in the Western world before 1960, if one were Roman Catholic, the local parish priest was the authority – he was even a minor god - for all questions and answers pertaining to morals, faith and religious practice. As early as I can remember, about 1950, when I was six years of age, until the early 1960's, my Sundays were quite predictable. The whole family dressed in their Sunday best to *religiously* attend Mass. Except for the sermon, the whole Mass was celebrated in Latin. I guess that was God's language of choice. Oddly enough, being raised in that tradition, we simply accepted that Latin was the way it would be. Forever! It wasn't until after the Second Vatican Council, which ended in 1965, that the Mass was begun to be celebrated in the vernacular, the language of the people, rather than in Latin. To my knowledge, most Catholics did little critical thinking for themselves. It was the Pope's, Cardinal's, Bishop's and parish priest's responsibility.

Prayer was mostly the prescribed repetition of specific prayers: The Lord's Prayer, the Hail Mary, the Glory Be, the Rosary and the Mass every Sunday as well as some weekdays.

From the age of six I was an inveterate sinner, or so I was led to believe. The rest of my family, and almost the whole congregation was incorrigible too. We all went to confession almost every week. Then everyone participated in Holy Communion weekly, with mandatory fasting: no food or drink from midnight until after Mass was concluded the next day.

In addition to the Sunday Mass there was regular daily Mass – which we attended occasionally - at 8:00 A.M. And summer vacation catechism classes instructed by the Sisters of Service. About the age of eight I was taught the Latin responses to the Mass and became an altar boy along with my brother, two of my cousins and a couple other neighbourhood kids. The job of the altar boys was to assist the priest in various ways as well as, on behalf of the congregation, to respond to the prayers and invocations of the priest. We used altar boy prayer cards with the Latin responses on the left half of the page and the English translation on the right side of the page, so we would have some idea as to what we were saying. Invariably, not being well versed in Latin pronunciation, and not knowing the meaning, we mumbled through many of the Latin responses. Hopefully God was good at interpreting our garbled efforts.

My earliest remembrances of God, religion, prayer, worship and devotion were rigidity, prescription and repetition together with a blend of love and fear. Those ideas are difficult to eradicate, some of them remaining with me till today. I learned that I had better practise all the rituals and prayer formulae taught to me or I stood an excellent chance of going to Hell. And the priests, nuns and my elders told me that was a bad place where you burned in everlasting fire that does not go out. Forgive me, but my primary view of God was this "Old White-Bearded Guy" in Heaven looking down on me, and all mankind, watching our every move, writing it all down and keeping track of our every transgression so that He can throw it all in our faces the moment we kick the proverbial bucket. Sort of scary, this "god" of my own creation (maybe I got a little help from my elders). Not at all like Meister Eckhart says, "The eye with which I see God is the same eye with which God sees me: my eye and God's eye are one eye, one seeing, one knowing, and one love." For me, God was much more as described by comedian George Carlin, "Religion has actually convinced people that there is an invisible man living in the sky, who watches everything you do, every minute of every day. And the invisible man has a special list of these ten things he does not want you to do. And if you do any of these ten things he has a special place full of fire and smoke and burning and torture and anguish where he will send you to live and suffer and burn and choke and cry and scream forever and ever 'til the end of time. - But he loves you."

Ah, you smirk at all this, but at catechism I was taught that for Catholics there were many more than ten infractions that could doom me forever. Protestants had it much easier. For instance, they did not have to attend Mass every Sunday; but then, according to many priests, their chance of getting to heaven was much more remote because the Catholic Church was the one true religion and those who followed its teachings, precepts and sacraments were the ones who would be first in line at the pearly gates. At times this attitude contributed to feelings of superiority and pride, not what would be categorized as virtues, in Catholic parishioners. The Catholic Church was full every Sunday. As far as I could surmise, most Catholics were there - maybe not out of the love of God, but rather, fear of Hell.

It was quite uncommon for Roman Catholics to participate in any way in Protestant religious services. I recall one situation where a child aged six died tragically as a result of a forty-five gallon steel drum tipping over and crushing him as he rode in the box of a pick-up truck – in those days there were no such things as seat belts and people regularly rode in the back of half ton trucks with no real safety concerns. Being just a few years older than the deceased, I was asked to be a pallbearer at the funeral. Since the funeral would be held in the local United Church, my parents consulted with the local parish priest and were advised that I could attend the funeral, but that I should not participate by being a pallbearer. I remember attending the funeral and feeling quite uncomfortable because, you know, *they prayed all wrong.* They didn't say the "Hail Mary" prayer after the Lord's Prayer and *that was just wrong.* I fixed it though. I said a silent "Hail Mary" while they prayed something else. Since that event I have often thought about the ridiculousness of the whole situation, and I have had guilty feelings about not fully participating in the young fellow's funeral, even though I was too young to know any better or to have a say in the matter.

Our whole family attended Mass every Sunday dressed in our Sunday best. In fact, my parents were so serious about Sunday Mass attendance that if, for some reason, there was no Mass in our local St. Helen's Roman Catholic Parish in Kuroki, Saskatchewan, my parents were sure to find an alternative. Sometimes we would attend a Mass at the local Ukrainian Catholic Church where the Mass was much longer, generally close to two hours in duration, conducted, not in Latin, but in the Old Slavonic language – another of God's favourite languages - which none of us understood. And the sermon was in Ukrainian, which was Greek to me. Apparently, some of the regular Ukrainian parishioners also regarded the Mass as of an excessive duration. During Mass we would observe certain adults with a nicotine habit sneaking out for a cigarette right in the middle of the religious ceremonies. The priest didn't call a recess, so they just took a smoke break.

Not to be too critical of the traditional Ukrainian Catholic Service! In some ways, to my youthful, curious mind, it was a pleasant change from our Latin Mass. The rituals were always elaborate with an abundance of incense, colourful vestments, together with processions displaying inspirational banners and icons - much ritual as well as a surfeit of pageantry. I shall never forget the Cantor leading the chanting and the melodic responses from the whole congregation. But more on my Ukrainian Catholic experiences later.

My brother Don and I sometimes tried to talk our way out of attending the Ukrainian Mass, but our parents were strict about attending a Catholic Mass *somewhere* every

Sunday. As a result, if there were no Catholic Mass in town, they would pack the family into our old Chevy and travel to the closest town where we could fulfil our Sunday obligation. Whether it was for love of our Creator or to avoid the mortal sin of missing Mass on Sunday, our whole family attended Mass every Sunday whether we liked it or not, unless one of us was on our deathbed, or near to it. I recall feeling quite a guilty pleasure about missing Mass on a couple of occasions, once when I had the Mumps and another time when I had the German measles.

In addition to the Sunday obligation, there were, and still are, "Holy Days of Obligation", days on which Catholics are obliged to attend Mass. In Canada there are currently only two Holy Days which do not fall on a Sunday: Christmas Day and the Feast of Mary, Mother of God. But back in the "olden days", the 1950's, there seemed to be many more days of obligation. The Catholic theory seemed to be that if the Church makes a rule that one *must* do something, apparently God's people will love God more.

One such obligation was Halloween. On October 31 every year there was an evening Mass usually about 7 or 7:30 P.M. for All Hallows Eve, the evening before All Saints Day on November 1. But that was also the night of trick or treat: only once a year when goblins can go door-to-door begging for treats. To my consternation, as well as that of my brother and our cousin, our parents insisted that the three of us attend evening church services before going out for our treats. We dutifully complied, as if we had any real choice. By the time we got out of church and hurried home to rush into our costumes and scurry through the darkened streets of Kuroki, all the other kids in town were finished their begging and had picked up all the good stuff.

We were the only kids in town performing the ritual trick-or-treating after 8:30 P.M. And we were naive enough to wonder why, despite our fabulous disguises, everyone could identify us. I'm sure it had nothing to do with the fact that year after year we always wore the same costumes, year after year the three of us haunted the streets together, and year after year we were the late comers. And we were likely the only three, having attended the evening Mass, to sport halos above our costumes.

The sacraments of the Eucharist (Holy Communion) and Confirmation were another issue, at least for me. The tradition of the church is that children are introduced to Holy Communion when they reach the age of reason, usually around the second grade. What about those of us who have received Holy Communion since the age of seven, are now seventy-five years old, but still haven't reached the age of reason? I'm slightly dubious about my own first Communion. Maybe I hadn't reached the age of reason. I'm sure it was a beautiful ceremony, but I seem to have missed the significance of receiving Christ's Body for the first time. Receiving Christ in the form of bread and wine, I was told, should be a sacrament of love, a remembrance of Jesus' sacrifice as He brought us "The Good News". Unfortunately, since at the time of my first communion we were not allowed to eat or drink from midnight until after the Mass was concluded, I recall having other things on my mind. First, the Sisters of Service, who taught us catechism and tried to help our juvenile minds comprehend the great mystery of the Eucharist, somehow impressed on me that I should be careful not to have the communion Host stick to the roof of my mouth. This was a real problem. With a very dry mouth (nothing to drink from bedtime until after Mass the next day) and a very dry Communion wafer, children sometimes panicked when the Communion Host stuck to the roof of their mouth. Second, it becomes more difficult to meditate on and appreciate God's goodness and love when one is suffering hunger pangs. God probably had a good chuckle when I prayed that I would get a nice big ham sandwich after Mass.

I was likely too young for the sacrament of Confirmation too. The Nuns who taught us catechism, preparing us for the sacrament, told us we should select a saint, one whom we admired, could relate to or aspire to emulate. When the bishop confirmed us, he would give us the name of this saint with whom we would be bonded spiritually, and to whom we could turn for guidance and protection. At the time of my confirmation my father owned Kuroki Hotel. His bartender was named Paul Pfroeschner. I chose St. Paul as my confirmation saint. Coincidence? I think not. Since my confirmation, particularly more recently, I have learned more about St Paul's experiences, devotion to and enthusiasm for Christ. I am proud to have St Paul as my protector. Maybe he's not so proud to be mine.

Then there was the practice/tradition/rule of not eating meat on Friday. It was established for Catholics as a reminder that Christ died on a Friday. The web site catholicism.org provides the following explanation: "Just why DO Catholics eat fish on Friday – or, better said why Catholics abstain from warm-blooded flesh meat on Friday? The obvious answer that every Catholic should know is that it is a penance imposed by the Church to commemorate the day of the Crucifixion of Our Lord – to enable us to make a small sacrifice for the incredible sacrifice He made for our salvation. Why, then, is fish allowed? The drawing of a symbolic fish in the dirt was a way that the early Christians knew each other when it was dangerous to admit in public that one was Christian. Our Lord cooked fish for His Apostles after His Resurrection, and most of these men were fishermen. After He established His Church, these fishermen became "fishers of men" for the Kingdom of God."

Fish on Fridays is a fine tradition, and fish is known to be a healthful food, but my recollection of the practice was somewhat different. I recall debates between adults and the parish priest about what foods could be eaten on Friday, and whether or not there were exceptions to the rule. Ducks spend much of their time on water. So, is it permissible to eat wild duck meat on Friday? What about whale or dolphin flesh? Or maybe platypus! When one travels a long distance, eating in restaurants, it is sometimes difficult to obtain fish on Fridays. Is it permissible to eat meat on these occasions? And when one is sick, deficient in iron, is meat eating on Fridays permissible? Seems to me we were looking for loopholes rather than trying to follow the intent of the rule. Once more, if the Church makes a rule that one *must* do something, apparently God's people will love God more. In Canada, the "fish on Fridays" rule is no longer practised except for the Ash Wednesday and Good Friday remembrances, so I guess we'll be working on finding devious methods of bending other church rules.

In reviewing the traditions, practices, teachings and indoctrination of my formative years I sometimes wonder how my religious and spiritual formative years influenced my view of God and religion. Almost all children are raised in the religious or spiritual traditions of their parents without ever being exposed to or educated about the spiritual beliefs, agnosticism or atheism of others. Does this contribute to bigotry, discrimination and narrow-mindedness? Perhaps a study of spirituality, the *Golden Rule*, and worldwide religious traditions as well as agnosticism and atheism might be offered as part of every person's formal education. Would society gain or lose by adopting this policy?

The weekend tradition of Latin Catholic Mass attendance continued until I completed my tenth grade. Kuroki was quite small, a hamlet of only 150 people together with numerous stray dogs and cats, therefore not large enough to have grades eleven and twelve in the local school. At that point, my parents gave me the choice of riding the school bus fifteen miles each way to a high school in Wadena, or of attending a Ukrainian Catholic boarding school, St. Joseph's College in Yorkton, Saskatchewan. I carefully weighed my options. My cousin, who had attended the "Good Ole' St Joes" for one year, advised me that St Joseph's College had a smoking room for the students. That certainly made my decision easier. I chose St. Joseph's College in Yorkton which was operated by the Ukrainian order of the Christian Brothers. There I continued my off and on relationship with Craven A cigarettes as well as a more in-depth exposure to the Ukrainian Catholic Mass and rituals.

Chapter 5
Український католик
(Ukrainian Catholic)

"I have a theory that if you've got the kind of parents who want to send you to boarding school, you're probably better off at boarding school" - Wendy Cope

In 1959 my life was changing. Having lived at home and attended the protected environment of the little red brick Kuroki School all my life, I was forced to grow up. There was no schooling beyond grade 10 in the tiny hamlet of Kuroki. For my eleventh and twelfth grades my parents gave me the option of attending St. Joseph's College, in Yorkton, Saskatchewan, about 75 miles from my hometown of Kuroki. St. Joseph's, operated by the Ukrainian Order of Christian Brothers, was a boarding school primarily for Ukrainian Catholic boys, but they accepted Latin Catholic students as well as a few

Protestants. Did my parents assume that all youth in attendance there would be exemplary goal-oriented students with high ideals and Christian values? Did they hope that I would internalize these values? Or did my parents believe that I was an incorrigible juvenile delinquent needing the regimentation of a boy's school? Maybe I should have asked, but I was naive and knew there were only two options: ride the school bus to and from Wadena, Saskatchewan over dusty roads for about an hour daily, or attend a boy's boarding school in Yorkton.

As previously mentioned, my difficult decision was made easier by the fact that my cousin had attended Ole' St. Joe's the previous year for his grade eleven. He informed me that St. Joe's permitted smoking in the school yard. But Saskatchewan winters can be harsh; so rather than trying to prevent students from smoking, the Christian Brothers provided a smoking room within the boarding school. In the 1950's it was the Christian thing to do. Students *needed* a place for recess, after class card playing and polluting their lungs with what we called cancer sticks, even back then. In the autumn of 1959, at the mature age of fifteen I knew that I had to take the smoking option rather than the daily dusty school bus option.

Naively, even though I certainly was not up for a halo nomination, I somehow imagined that St. Joseph's College would be a little utopia, a sacred island, a saintly Eden, uniquely sheltered from the heathen mobs outside those walls. Everyone there would be exemplary Christians, or at least be amenable to embrace Christian values: love God and love your neighbour. Sure, all students took religion classes, and all students attended Mass at the Ukrainian Catholic Church each Sunday. As well, there were daily weekday Masses in the College Chapel, but these were mostly optional. It didn't take me long to learn that Catholic high school students, Ukrainian or not, were subject to the same temptations, foibles and human failings as students everywhere else in the world. And the teachers, bless their Christian Brother hearts, were human too. I saw, heard via the grapevine, and sometimes personally experienced cursing, temper tantrums, bullying, cheating, harassment and surreptitious alcohol consumption on the part of some teachers and some students.

The bullying was primarily a student phenomenon. There was a "briar patch", an extremely thorny hedge in a green space or park area just east of the college. It contained a ball diamond, skating rink, open space of a few acres and the dreaded briar patch. I had heard of an informal hazing ritual some new students were subjected to by the most vicious of the bullies. The prospective victims had their shirts forcibly removed from their backs; then they were dragged feet first, with their bare backs being scraped and shredded, through the thorn hedge. Must have been a Christian ritual; Christ was forced to wear a crown of thorns at his crucifixion; so, some deranged students must have felt it was appropriate to inflict thorns on certain novices. I never saw anyone being subjected to this torture, but I had heard about it, cringed at the thought of it, and feared that it would happen to me.

One pleasant Sunday afternoon in late September, shortly after the beginning of the school year, one of my new friends and I were lying in the park just adjacent to the dreaded thorn hedge. A large hairy brute of a student joined us, visited for a few minutes, and then for some reason decided that I should be subjected to the thorn hedge. His threatening manner gave me pause. I was not sure how to react: to run, fight or simply resign myself to the inevitable. The brute was a foot taller than me and outweighed me by at least forty pounds. I am forever grateful to my quick-thinking new friend who had attended St Joe's the previous year. He lied for me, telling the bully that I had already received my thorny initiation on the week of my arrival. Somehow, that placated him, resulting in a bestowal of mercy on me and my tender body.

It was not until a couple weeks later that I discovered how lucky I really was to avoid that informal hazing. In St. Joe's we could not take a shower anytime we wanted or needed it. Every Friday night was shower night, whether we needed it or not. *We needed it!* All one hundred and forty or so students had their shower on the same night, starting with the oldest, the grade twelve students, and working down to the youngest, the grade nines. There were ten shower stalls in the basement of the old college. We were herded down there, 20 students at a time. Each group of ten made their way to the shower stalls while the next ten in line stood shivering with their towels wrapped around them. When the first ten entered the showers, the countdown began with our prefect, Brother Josephat, timing the whole event. Each group was entitled to five minutes of water, then a couple minutes to towel dry before the next ten in line got their turn. The whole ablution ceremony was carried out with military precision. Trying to get well over one hundred showers accomplished on the same evening often resulted in the water heaters not being able to handle the volume of water required, with the consequence that many of the later groups were subjected to lukewarm, or even ice-cold showers. Some students gossiped that it was a deliberate plot to stifle the libido of the mobs of pubescent male students. But I digress - more on our hormones later.

It turned out that within the group of ten waiting in line with me was Stephen, a boy from Chicago, sent to Yorkton, Saskatchewan, Canada by his widowed mother to receive a good Christian education at the hands of the Christian Brothers. When it came our turn to shower, Stephen dropped the towel from his back to reveal dried blood, scabs and painful gouges from his waistline up to his neck. He had evidently been dragged through the briar patch. Our Prefect, Brother Josephat, scowling at the sight, angrily demanded, "Who did this to you?" The code of silence prevailed. Stephen apparently didn't want to be the "rat fink" in spite of his very obvious pain. The next day Stephen was ushered into the Director's office for an interrogation, but to my knowledge he never revealed the identity of his tormentor. The perpetrator of the hazing went unpunished, but the reaction of Brother Josephat may have been enough to dissuade repeat offences. During the remainder of my stay at St Joe's I never heard of another hazing. Less egregious bullying, name calling, and harassment were more common.

The teachers, for the most part, seemed to be devout Christians, setting a good example for their charges. They had daily Mass, group prayers and, as far as I could discern, they were generally pious. In fact, one was named Brother Pius. They were good teachers who sometimes became frustrated, disappointed and angry at the laziness and intransigence of many students. One teacher in particular, who shall remain unnamed, frequently cursed a blue streak when he became upset. On one occasion he created quite a spectacle when presenting us with the results of one of our mathematics quizzes. The class average was so poor that, as he entered the classroom, he let loose a stream of temper, invective and cursing quite inappropriate for any teacher, let alone a Christian Brother.

It went something like this: upon entering the room, he threw our marked test papers on his desk and kicked the army-green metal wastebasket, strewing its contents across the room. His face turning beet-red, either from a well-rehearsed show of rage or from very obvious anger, he shouted words to this effect, "Piss on you sailors! You sons of bitches never did a stitch of work to prepare for this exam."

In contrast with the bullying, cheating, cursing and clandestine alcohol consumption, as far as I knew there were no sexual dalliances except in the minds of the teenage boys attending St Joe's. In fact, we rarely saw girls. Sacred Heart Academy, a Ukrainian Catholic boarding school for girls was only a few blocks away, but St. Joseph's College students, unless receiving permission to go there for a specific purpose, were strictly forbidden to venture within one block of the Academy. The Nuns who oversaw and taught the teenage girls ensured this edict was enforced. There were only a few occasions when the two sexes could venture within hailing distance of one another. One such instance was at Sunday Mass when we attended St. Mary's Ukrainian Catholic Church, just one block from our school.

There, the girls of Sacred Heart Academy sat in the pews on one side of aisle, carefully watched by the eagle-eyed nuns. The boys from St. Joseph's sat on the other side of the aisle, nervously sneaking side-glances at the distant, elusive objects of their affection whilst trying not to attract the attention of the ever-watchful Christian Brothers. After Mass, a few of the bolder guys – I was not one of them - ventured a short visit with one or two of the girls, attempting to arrange a Saturday afternoon tryst. Then the boys were all herded back to the College and the girls paraded back to the Academy to eat Sunday brunch. The Christian Brothers kept us on a short leash. Saturday afternoon was one of the few times we were free to go downtown. Except for what we called our "free time", Wednesday afternoons, and then again on Saturday afternoon and Saturday evening until 11:00 pm, we were not permitted to leave the college grounds and surrounding area. The girls were kept on a tighter rein, only being given freedom on Saturday afternoons.

One other occasion when the two sexes had a chance to intermingle was the very infrequent dance, once or twice a year, overseen by the drill-sergeant nuns and platoon commander Christian Brothers. The boys sat on one side of the dance hall, the girls on the other. Having had negligible opportunity to become acquainted prior to the dance, only the very brave did much dancing. I took refuge in the massive stag line along with the other social misfits. On a few occasions I worked up the courage to ask a pretty girl to dance but having two left feet and a raging case of acne did little to boost my confidence on the dance floor or in any other social interactions. On one occasion, leaving the stag line, I made the trek across the dance floor. Nothing gained! After being rejected, I trudged back, with all eyes on me, grudgingly accepting a lesson in shame and humility.

Near the end of my second and final year at St Joe's, one pleasant Saturday morning in May, Brother Pius asked me to go for a walk in the woods just a few blocks from the school. I wondered at that but accepted his invitation. After strolling and making small talk for ten minutes or so, he popped the question: "Had I ever considered becoming a Christian Brother?" Somewhat surprised by his question, I confided in him that I had given it a fleeting thought, but I was not seriously considering it. He suggested that I think and pray about it and discuss it with him further. I told him I would do that, but my thoughts about the option were more along the lines of, "How do I say, 'No'?" and "Am I saying no to a call from God?" Being a typical Catholic, I was wracked with guilt feelings about my decision to decline. Moreover, there were peripheral reasons why I felt some pressure to accede to his suggestion. One of my first cousins was already in the priesthood, his sister from the same family had taken vows as a nun, and one of his brothers who was my age, was seriously considering the novitiate to the priesthood. Was I the black sheep? Probably!

Being seventeen years old at the time, with my hormones raging, I did not see myself taking or being capable of living a vow of celibacy. With that implication, but not in those precise words, the next time we met, I advised Brother Pius of my decision. I could see the disappointment in his face, but to this day I am certain I made the right choice.

Speaking of libido and hormones, several students started the rumour that the Christian Brothers had instructed the cooks to lace our food with saltpetre, or as is known by its chemical name, potassium nitrate. Saltpetre is a common food preservative and additive, fertilizer, and oxidizer for fireworks and rockets. There is an unsubstantiated belief that ingesting saltpetre will lower the libido. I seriously doubt that any non-nutritive additives were placed in our food. Besides, if the attempt had been made, it would have been to no avail. There is little that will inhibit the libido of teenage boys. However, the rumour persisted and was believed by many. Fake news existed in the 1950's, long before the launching of the internet and social media.

As I leave my reminiscences of old St. Joe's I ask myself, "Would open classroom discussions of the *Golden Rule* in relation to initiation rites, bullying, hazing and other abusive situations help to reduce painful, and sometimes criminal behaviour? Would application of the *Golden Rule* guide educational and judicial authorities in the application of appropriate discipline in abusive situations?"

With my graduation from St. Joseph's College in June of 1961, at the age of seventeen, I thought I was all grown up, mature, and ready for all that life could throw at me. Further, I was pretty much a Catholic (maybe not a good one), but after two years of exposure to the Ukrainian Catholic Mass and rituals, I felt quite at home with the Ukrainian Catholics.

Chapter 6
Erotic Encounters

"In opposition to sex education: Let the kids today learn it where we did – in the gutter."
- Pat Paulson

In contrast with the religious indoctrination afforded me and my siblings, the topic of sex was pretty well taboo. Sex did not exist during the 1950's. At least not any about which adults informed me! That doesn't mean they weren't doing it. They just didn't talk about it. Almost no one had television. Some didn't even have electricity. Adults were doing something during the long, dark winter nights as evidenced by the families of four to nine children or more during the post-World War 2 era. But as far as I was informed by adults, including my parents, the mother became larger, until she went to the hospital where the stork brought her a baby. That was it! I wasn't completely stupid. I knew Santa Claus was real, but storks bringing babies was a little far-fetched. Knowing something fishy was happening is one thing, but never getting information directly from "anyone actively engaged in coitus", as Sheldon from the *Big Bang Theory* might remark, is another thing. Sure, I always got sprinklings of information on the dusty streets of Kuroki from boys a few years older who had gleaned juicy titbits from their older sisters or brothers. They knew a modicum about the facts of life and were eager to play the role of sex educator by sharing the secret with us youngsters. And they told us crude, juvenile jokes about "the wiener going into the bun". Farm boys were a great source of information too. For them, it was natural, a part of raising cattle. They helped their parents and couldn't help but see the bull having intimate relations with the heifers, the roosters ruffling the feathers of the hens and the rams getting cosy with the ewes. Then, several months later, as part of their education, they would often see the birth of calves or lambs.

Even for small town children there were methods of discovering differences in the sexes. Ample evidence existed in the undergarments pages of Sears Mail Order Catalogues. Doesn't take a rocket scientist or a gynaecologist to notice sexual differences! Pregnant women were a common sight; yet we didn't see any pregnant men. Frequently, women openly breast fed their infants. But nobody – except, perhaps pre-teens, teens and joking males in bars – openly talked about sex, sexual urges or sexual differences.

The confusing part about all this secrecy is that it made the whole topic even more intriguing. Things were happening to my body, even before puberty. I don't want to talk about this – I've been trained not to - but in all honesty,

I had my first lover when I was six years old. Yep, and she was about seventeen or eighteen. The age difference was no factor. Besides, it only happened in a dream. It was my first "nocturnal emission". I do not recall being attracted to the young lady in any way or, perhaps I should call her the old lady when I compare her age at the time to my age at the time. The whole affair was completely innocent, at least on my part. But somehow during the night she ravished me. I still fondly recall her vivid ruby red lipstick, her warm, soft body against mine and the very moment when our two hearts and bodies became one. At that age, I knew almost nothing about the female anatomy, so in my dream – it was a night dream, not a daydream – she has a penis. That was of no significance to me. I just knew that the experience was pleasurable, but I knew not what it all meant, never revealing my first sexual encounter until this very day. By now that young lady is either about eighty-five years old, or she is resting peacefully in her grave without her six-year-old molester pestering her for sexual favours in his dreams. She will remain unnamed.

    The next year, at the age seven, I had the opportunity of a lifetime, which I declined. A couple of my female childhood friends invited a few of us boys over for a "tea party". There were five of us, three boys and two girls. After the tea party the girls invited the boys over to the municipal storage yard where there were several huge galvanized steel culverts awaiting their placement on some new grid roads. The girls' suggestion was that "we'll show you ours, if you show us yours". Two of the boys took them up on their generous offer. For some reason, which I do not recall – perhaps my parents had cautioned me about such dalliances, or maybe I was just too nervous – I missed the free anatomy lesson. In any event, the result was rather amusing. When the proposed exploratory exchange of "peek at my pubic parts" was complete, the boys emerged from the culverts grinning from ear to ear. Even though I was too shy to partake in the adventure, I certainly wanted to hear about it.

"Benny, what happened in there? Did you see anything?" I inquired.

"Nah, there's nothing to see. They pulled their panties down, and we had a look. But they have nothing but a crack down there," Benny replied.

"Yeah?" I continued, rather incredulous, "So then, did you show them yours?"

"Nah!" Benny retorted. "Once we had a look at theirs, we just took off."

Children will always be innocently curious. But there were other learning experiences, some of which would now be classified as sexual abuse, misdemeanours or sexual misconduct. These all occurred when I was between the ages of eight and fourteen. One incident, bordering on paedophilia, scandalized our tiny community. Then there were a few credible (perhaps incredible!) reports of bestiality as well as rumours of wife-swapping in a neighbouring town. These incidents shall remain generic to avoid re-traumatizing innocent victims and relatives still alive.

In another questionable affair, when I was nine years old, as several of us sat around visiting, a boy about fourteen years old was so proud of the size of his erect penis he invited a few of us who were younger to feel it through his blue jeans. Finally – males might be familiar with this occurrence – on long, dark winter evenings at the skating rink, one would often hear the older teens bragging about their conquests, real or imagined, of the previous weekend.

What is most interesting about all these incidents is that adults almost never discussed sexual matters with their children, at least not that I heard of, and especially not in our family. Somehow, it seems to me, that my parents didn't know what to say to me. Then I didn't know what to say to my son. And so, we continue, generation after generation with almost no sex education except that learned on the streets and in the gutters. I know that no children should receive their education on sensitive personal matters from their peers, or – heaven forbid – from internet porn sites. Yet that is what is happening. This discourse, or lack of it, regarding sexual matters in conjunction with traditional puritan religious attitudes appears to be having profound negative implications for society in general as well as for many religions and the leaders of those religions, to say nothing of the scandals surrounding powerful political leaders and heads of major businesses and corporations.

Many years ago, Doctor Benjamin Spock said, *"Sex education, including its spiritual aspects, should be part of a broad health and moral education from kindergarten through grade twelve, ideally carried out harmoniously by parents and teachers."* Would the implementation of Dr. Spock's recommendation facilitate the use of the *Golden Rule* by parents, educators and pastors to illustrate relevant information about appropriate sexual conduct? Could it also reduce the indiscretions and crimes which have given rise to the *"Me Too"* movement?

Chapter 7
Political Naivety

Politics is the art of looking for trouble, finding it everywhere, diagnosing it incorrectly and applying the wrong remedies. - Groucho Marx

Contrary to my indoctrination into Catholicism and the mysterious silence surrounding anything sexual, I often heard adults become rather heated about politics. Growing up in Kuroki Hotel in the 1950's, I was exposed to politics in the raw. The heated political discussions in the beer parlour fuelled by liberal (no pun intended) quantities of beer tended to exacerbate political rifts which occasionally spilled out onto the street or into the hotel café/dining room for curious little ears to overhear. I didn't see any fist fights over politics, but I certainly heard some loud voices. Occasionally my father would get involved in some of these heated discussions, but to his credit, I would hear him discuss issues and propose solutions rather than providing blind partisan support to just one political party. Secondhand exposure to barroom politics helped me to understand that if not everyone agrees on the best way forward in the tiny community of Kuroki, solutions to international problems were even more elusive.

In 1956, when I was in the sixth grade, we studied and discussed current events in our Social Studies class. Memories of the Second World War, the bloodiest in history, just ending in 1945, were still fresh in the minds of most adults. The Cold War was in vogue. A new Hot War seemed imminent. In class we talked about the threat of nuclear attack from the Soviet Union and why one should stay away from windows if a hydrogen bomb were dropped. Flying glass was a definite threat. We also learned that if one looked directly at a nuclear blast the result would likely be blindness caused by burned retinas. We were coached to hide under our school desks to avoid being hurt or killed by falling debris when the aftershock hit our school. To us, and to most of North America, the threat was very real. In my youthful, innocent mind, I knew there was an easy solution. I remember naively suggesting to the teacher that the leaders of the USSR and the USA, being the most powerful nations in the world, simply had to get together and agree to keep peace in the world. Isn't that what they both want? Isn't that what their citizens want? Isn't that what the world wants? The teacher told me that was not possible. The difference in the politics of the two countries was too great. *Was it?* I was incredulous. As kids on the playground we were told to play fair, not to bully, to share things rather than being greedy. For adult relationships and countries solving their issues, it seems there were different rules. How could the two most powerful countries on earth not want peace? In today's world it is even more difficult because now there are three major nuclear powers – China, Russia and the United States of America, as well as several others with nuclear capability, or working toward it. I still believe that if the three most powerful countries worked together – seems I'm still naïve - they could drastically reduce armaments and improve the chances for peace in the whole world. Apparently, it won't happen. Humans appear to thrive on conflict and power struggles. One of the most lucrative global industries is the military industrial complex. Each of the three major powers either openly or surreptitiously supports rogue regimes around the world with bigger and better armaments. And each of those three countries idolizes its military, promoting their arms manufacturing industries. It is big business, which no one appears to be willing to repudiate. Around the globe, uncountable dollars are wasted annually on armaments which do nothing to promote world peace and security. Our political leaders are under the delusion that war and threats of war lead to peace; whereas, history has demonstrated that war leads to more war. Many people, much wiser than I, have shown how those trillions of dollars and millions of lives squandered in the manufacture and utilization of killing machines could be used to feed the hungry, clean the environment and provide free health care and education for the masses, all of which would lead to more peace.

There do not appear to be political or religious solutions to humanity's problems. In fact, western democracy's divisive politics and religion may be driving large numbers of people away from voting, from traditional political parties as well as from traditional religions.

To my recollection, that early social studies/current events classroom discussion was my first brush with politics and my first political disappointment. Certainly not my last! My naivety persists. The solution is still amazingly simple – it would not be easy, but it could be simple. We need leaders who do not promote fear and war, but leaders who promote peace and prosperity for all, not through more armaments, but through a serious reduction in the military of every country in the world. We need three wise men: brave, optimistic humanitarians – leaders of the three most militarily powerful countries on earth to agree to at least start a dialogue on the topic. Or maybe we need wise women. Men have been tried and they have been found wanting. We need leaders who do not seek to divide humanity, but rather leaders who recognize all humans as brothers and sisters – leaders who are willing to try the *Golden Rule*. We have had a few such leaders in John F. Kennedy, Martin Luther King, Mahatma Gandhi, Robert Kennedy and Nelson Mandela. But we vilified, jailed or assassinated them. The same was done to Jesus when he promoted the brotherhood of man, all people being sons and daughters of one God, loving our neighbours as ourselves. Was Jesus naive too?

Chapter 8
Political Suicide

"There never was a democracy yet that did not commit suicide." - John Quincy Adams

For several years, I paid little attention to international, national or regional politics. I was too young to care and there was no point. The teacher had told me there was no chance that the major powers could reach agreement to bring world peace. So why even think about politics? That attitude of denial lasted until about 1960 when I graduated from high school and was offered a summer job as the assistant secretary for the Rural Municipality of Sasman. Using a mechanical calculator, I calculated taxes for all properties within the municipality, balanced the tax rolls and sent out tax notices. Then I assisted the Municipal Secretary with the sometimes-interesting task of dealing with ratepayers as they came to the office to pay their taxes. Politics inevitably comes to the forefront when money is involved. Invariably, taxpayers contend that taxes are too high, and the level of services is too low. But these were minor disagreements and skirmishes, discussions between Tony, the municipal secretary, and the taxpayer, usually ending in an agreement to amicably disagree.

However, a political tsunami was on the horizon, making provincial politics in Saskatchewan controversial, highly charged and rather interesting. I sensed rumblings of it when farmers came in to pay taxes and to buy hail insurance on their crops. The social democratic party, the Co-operative Commonwealth Federation (CCF), in the June 8, 1960 election, had defeated the opposition Liberal party by taking 37 of the 54 seats in the provincial legislature. The CCF had campaigned with a promise to provide taxpayer-funded universal health care. I had been too young to vote, but I heard it all. Ratepayers came down on both sides of the issue, some siding with the proposed legislation of universal health care and others siding with the doctors, the majority of whom were vehemently opposed to the legislation, with the College of Physicians and Surgeons telling voters that Medicare would take freedom of choice away from patients and would cause doctors to leave the province. There was even talk of a protest strike by doctors, with epic battle lines being drawn between social-democrats and conservatives.

It takes time to draft new legislation, and even more time to revamp procedures, payment systems and guidelines for doctors and patients when introducing a radical change in the operation of provincial health care. But it happened on July 1, 1962. And the doctors immediately went on strike from July 1 until July 23, 1962. By the end of the second week of the strike, several British, American and Canadian doctors arrived in Saskatchewan to provide medical services withheld by local physicians. As the tension mounted, there were acts of violence and threats of blood in the streets. At an anti-Medicare rally, a Roman Catholic priest, Father Athol Murray, gave a speech which further inflamed sentiment by saying, "This thing may break into violence and bloodshed any day now, and God help us if it doesn't." This was only one of the incendiary speeches Murray had made throughout the province, causing the Catholic Church to order him out of the province until the whole issue was more settled. Tempers finally cooled on July 23, 1962 when the College of Physicians and Surgeons called off the strike after an arrangement with the government, known as the Saskatoon Agreement. The agreement included some compromises and ambiguities; however, the main point of the agreement was that medical insurance would remain government controlled, compulsory, universal and reasonably comprehensive. As the plan became more widely known and more popular, there was pressure to make it available to all citizens of Canada. There was no turning back.

On December 8, 1966, The National Medical Care Insurance Act was passed in Canada's House of Commons in Ottawa by a landslide vote of 177 to 2. The start date of the plan was July 1, 1968, with the Act providing that the federal government would pay about half of Medicare costs in any province with insurance plans that met the criteria of being universal, publicly administered, portable and comprehensive. By 1971 all provinces had established plans which met those criteria.

The history of the implementation of universal medical services in Canada together with the ongoing divisive debate in the USA leads me to wonder about this issue in relation to Christianity. Jesus' ministry involved curing the body as well as the spirit. Have Christian religious zealots forgotten one-half of the equation? Furthermore, have politicians' emphasis on winning re-election and their focus on party platforms rather than on the *Golden Rule* and the needs of their constituents prevented our democracies from achieving excellence? Does oblivious extreme fervour for a religion or a political party cause moral blindness and spiritual paralysis?

Found on Facebook: "Cataract is the third biggest cause of blindness. Religion and politics remain the first two."

Part 2 - Exploration

"I don't pretend to have all the answers.

But the questions are certainly worth thinking about."

-- Arthur C. Clarke

Chapter 9
Accident or Design

"The whole war between the atheist and the theist comes down to this: the atheist believes a 'what' created the universe; the theist believes a 'who' created the universe." — Criss Jami, *Killosophy*.

I wonder what happened at the very beginning, before the universe began, before the world was formed, and before the miracle of life. We currently have two predominant ideas about *the theory of everything*. On the one hand we are told to accept the words of Genesis literally: "In the beginning God created the heavens and the earth. Now the earth was a formless void, there was darkness over the deep, and God's spirit hovered over the water. God said, 'Let there be light,' and there was light." In the beautiful narrative of Genesis, we are told how, in the following few days, God created everything that exists. On the other hand, we have the big bang theory, the leading scientific explanation about how the universe began. In essence, it tells us to believe the universe started with a small singularity – who or what initiated that *singularity* is left unanswered – which inflated over the next 13.8 billion years to the cosmos that we think we know today. (In fact, we really only know about an infinitesimally small fraction of it.) According to NASA, in the first second after the universe began, the surrounding temperature was about 10 billion degrees Fahrenheit or 5.5 billion degrees Celsius. We are told to believe that the cosmos contained a vast array of fundamental particles such as neutrons, electrons and protons. These decayed or combined as the universe got cooler. Then, from this primordial soup, over billions of years, emerged everything that now exists. I do not disbelieve this theory. It may have happened. My interest, however, is much more basic. If it did happen, who or what initiated that singularity?

I believe the whole debate between creationists and evolutionists is ridiculous. There are those who agree with both camps. Is it perhaps most likely that God began by giving us a jump-start by creating the *stuff* to begin the process: the atoms and the DNA? Then He created the laws of the universe: heat, light, magnetism and gravity; and their interaction through the sciences: physics, chemistry, biology, gravity, and even evolution – all the laws of nature. Evolution is a natural method of providing a species with means of adapting, adjusting and improving based on that species' needs relative to its interaction with the environment, other members of its own species and members of other species. Biologists, horticulturalists and scientists have proved that plants and animals do evolve. In fact, they have utilized evolutionary techniques to breed hardier, drought and disease resistant plants: flowers of amazing beauty; high yielding and tasty fruits, vegetables and grains. They have also selectively bred cattle, swine and sheep to develop animals with desired characteristics: cattle producing more milk or better beef, leaner hogs for better bacon and sheep with more abundant, softer wool. They have bred racehorses and draft horses with characteristics suited to the needs of man. They have bred all manner of dogs and cats with the size, appearance, aptitudes and demeanour desired by their masters.

One common proof often used by evolutionists is that genetic studies have shown that humans and chimpanzees share between 96 and 98 percent of their DNA. All living things have some commonality of DNA. In fact, according to getscience.com and several other scientific websites we share 50% common DNA with bananas. (There's a joke and a pun in there somewhere. I invite you to make one up to suit yourself.) If humans evolved from chimpanzees, where are the species/creatures on the continuum between humans and apes – did they just disappear into thin air? Maybe not! We have all known certain humans with ape-like manners and characteristics. My spouse accuses me, and yours probably accuses you too, of emitting certain odours which remind her of the zoo, but that is not proof of evolution.

All kidding aside! Evolution is a fact. It is just that Darwin carried his findings to an illogical conclusion. I doubt that a lizard ever turned into a rabbit, a fish into a fowl, or that an onion evolved into a human. Perhaps billions of years from now, if humanity does not blow itself to Kingdom Come in the interim, I will be proved wrong. Until then I can believe in evolution within a species, but I am not so eager to believe that one *species* can magically *evolve* into another. If it really does happen, *Someone* must cause it to be so. Yes, evolution is a fact. In my opinion, so is creation. It is just not possible to prove creation. Simple logic should be proof enough, but it obviously is not. In Stephen Hawking's last book, *Brief Answers to the Big Questions*, he emphatically states, "We are each free to believe what we want, and it's my view that the simplest explanation is that there is no God. No one created the universe, and no one directs our fate."

"Well, Stephen," - that's me addressing Stephen Hawking directly - "Someone did create the universe, but I can't debate you about that. I wish you luck in convincing God that He does not exist and did not create the universe."

Stephen Hawking was an intelligent person, but he did not know the answer to all the questions of our existence. Neither do I. Stephen could speculate. So can I. At times I may feel a little agnosticism, or maybe it is simply the *not knowing for sure*. It takes faith to be a believer. But the absolute wonder of nature and the universe as well as the miracle of life convince me that there must be much more than we can see and understand. The stuff, everything in all of existence, had to be started. In all my human experience and understanding, "Something" has never materialized out of "Nothing". "Something" or "Someone" must initiate an action to cause "Something" to "be". That "Someone" in my mind, is God, Supreme Being, Loving Force, Creator, Allah – always the same Creator known by different names depending upon one's religion, ethnicity, culture and upbringing. Maybe we know this to be true. But sometimes we need to be reminded of this absolute truth. Those of us who are Christian sometimes need reminding that God is evident in all the mysteries of nature, maybe even more so than in the Bible. One morning I was reminded of this miracle when I read Father Richard Rohr's daily meditation.

He tells us, "*All you have to do today is walk outside and gaze at one leaf, long and lovingly, until you know, really know that this leaf is a participation in the eternal being of God. It's enough to create ecstasy.*"

Canadian poet and author Bliss Carman (1861 – 1929) creates a similar image in his poem *Vestigia**, while going one step farther by recognizing that if we really search, we will find the essence of God within our hearts.

Vestigia

I took a day to search for God,
And found Him not. But as I trod
By rocky ledge, through woods untamed,
Just where one scarlet lily flamed,
I saw His footprint in the sod.

Then suddenly, all unaware,
Far off in the deep shadows, where
A solitary hermit thrush
Sang through the holy twilight hush—
I heard His voice upon the air.

And even as I marvelled how
God gives us Heaven here and now,
In a stir of wind that hardly shook
The poplar leaves beside the brook—
His hand was light upon my brow.

At last with evening as I turned
Homeward, and thought what I had learned
And all that there was still to probe—

I caught the glory of His robe
Where the last fires of sunset burned.

Back to the world with quickening start
I looked and longed for any part
In making saving Beauty be....
And from that kindling ecstasy
I knew God dwelt within my heart.

*Note: *Vestigia* is a poem in the public domain.

There is more, much more to cause me to bow my head in humbleness and awe. Commonplace, everyday experiences I mostly take for granted are given by our creator: the butterfly, the sunrise, the seasons, the amazing diversity of plant and animal, the night sky, the universe itself. Some things are so close to us, we cannot see them. Our brain. Our eyeball. The intricacy, beauty and functioning of the human brain and eyeball are daily miracles. The eye is a unique, complex and amazing organ, transmitting colour, movement, light and perspective to the brain which interprets thousands of bits of information our every waking minute. Do I enjoy and thank God for the kaleidoscope of colour I see every day? Just ask a person who was blind, suddenly having their sight restored. The bible recounts at least four instances of Jesus providing the miracle of sight to blind people. Most of us enjoy the miracle of sight every day of our lives without ever giving thanks. God's creations, His blessings and miracles often go unrecognized and unappreciated until they are taken away.

When it comes to the mysteries of creation and evolution, I know very little and I am certain of nothing. But I tend toward the words of the late John McCain, *"I believe in evolution. But I also believe, when I hike the*

Grand Canyon and see it at sunset, that the hand of God is there also."

"Well, John," That's me talking to John McCain. "By now you will have felt the comforting, healing and forgiving hand of God. Peace be with you and yours."

Richard Rohr says: "God seems to have chosen to manifest the invisible in what we call the "visible," so that all things visible are the revelation of God's endlessly diffusive spiritual energy. Once a person recognizes that, it is hard to ever be lonely in this world again."

For the stubborn sceptic, the true atheist, this quotation by Sir Arthur Conan Doyle is worth considering: "Once you eliminate the impossible, whatever remains, no matter how improbable, must be the truth." When I considered this quotation in relation to the existence of the universe and all it contains, I know that it is impossible for these wonders to have created themselves, for them to have appeared just by accident, out of nothing. All that remains, for me, is a Creator – no matter how improbable, *that* must be the truth.

Should our educational systems present the theory of evolution in conjunction with the belief in creationism? Is there any reason why we should be afraid to consider both possibilities? In fact, could they both be *probabilities*?

Chapter 10
Man, the Manipulator

"All the great religions have a place for awe, for ecstatic transport at the wonder and beauty of creation." - Richard Dawkins

In the beautiful act of sexual intimacy, God has given fertile humans the power to create another human being, a unique being. There is no exact copy of us in the universe. That individuality begins way before we become a zygote, a fertilized egg in our mother's womb. Before we became part of the human race, a small part of us, the sperm from our father won the race to the egg. Under a powerful microscope, that race between human sperm looks just like a bunch of wriggling tadpoles. But it makes a monumental difference which sperm wins. Genetic studies have shown that even sperm cells from the same man have huge differences. Scientists have obtained genetic blueprints of almost 100 sperm from a single individual and they have discovered huge DNA differences in each of the individual sperms. Take a victory lap. You – or rather, your sperm progenitor – won the race. If one of those other wriggling tadpoles had won the sprint to the egg, would there be no *you*? Would there be someone else to experience the miracle of existence? Makes one wonder: are our lives a crap shoot? What part does chance play in our entire existence? Doubtful that God has an inventory of souls and minds, allocating them out in a specific order (or maybe that is the plan. Only God knows). We humans have the monumental responsibility, in partnership with our Creator, to initiate and cherish the uniqueness of human life. Perhaps that is why God instilled in parents such love of their children.

Many humans believe we are created in the image and likeness of God. It says so in the Bible. Genesis 1:26: "God said, 'Let us make man in our own image, in the likeness of ourselves ....'" We have been given many amazing qualities: the ability to learn, free will, the desire to create, and the ability to love. But we are not God. We are not creators. In this age of technology, artificial intelligence and super-computers, man has become prideful of his wondrous "creations". Humans have come to believe that they can achieve almost anything, that God is no longer necessary. The fact is, we can only manipulate what has already been created. Even our own thoughts, which we believe are original, our own "creation", have a source other than ourselves. Our brains, our brain cells and even our thought processes have not been created by us. For example, I felt pretty good when I wrote and published my first book, *Barking From the Front Porch*. In fact, I created nothing. I manipulated memories, thoughts and the written word into something I felt was worth sharing.

This is not to diminish the accomplishments of the brilliant scientists, astronomers, inventors, writers, artists, sculptors and composers who have manipulated what has already been created, fashioning it to look, feel or sound like a new creation. In humbleness, it is worth remembering and praising the Loving Source from which originates *everything*. Joyce Kilmer (1886-1918) succinctly reminds us of this fact in his poem *Trees*.

Trees
I think that I shall never see.
A poem lovely as a tree
A tree whose hungry mouth is prest
Against the earth's sweet flowing breast;
A tree that looks at God all day,
And lifts her leafy arms to pray;
A tree that may in summer wear
A nest of robins in her hair;
Upon whose bosom snow has lain;
Who intimately lives with rain.
Poems are made by fools like me,
But only God can make a tree.

It could be said that I split hairs on my definitions of creation and manipulation. But consider carefully, *only God can make a tree*. No human has ever created anything. We want to create. Being in God's likeness, we enjoy constructing, refashioning, manipulating the treasures of this earth into objects we regard as our own creations. Even children, from their earliest years, fashion crude creations which they eagerly and proudly display to their parents and friends. Imagine the pride of that little child coming home from kindergarten cradling her first creation, a crude drawing, a piece of art for Mom and Dad to hang on the refrigerator door. The child loves her creation. That same feeling exists in every artist, sculptor, dancer, carpenter, plumber, musician, or author – in every human being. The carpenter moulds, shapes, bends, cuts, nails and glues pieces of wood, which were once a tree, a beautiful creation, into a desk, cabinet or coffee table: a new beautiful creation. That same tree could be used by a sculptor or a carver to fashion a unique artistic creation. What the carpenter and the sculptor have created, they proudly display and love.

The composer or author can take a piece of blank paper, a creation made from that same tree, to imagine, to fashion, to dream, to compose yet another creation. There are only eight notes in music - plus some sharps and flats - and only twenty-six letters in the English alphabet. The obsession of every composer, lyricist and author is to fashion those few notes into billions of amazing melodies or to weave those few letters into uncountable creations of drama, mystery, comedy and tragedy yet untold. They do not write because they want to write; they write because they must write. Their obsession is to inspire, to elicit raw emotions - awe, love, ecstasy, glee, sorrow, fear, hate, sympathy or suspense. It is an invitation, for a moment, to escape from the routine of our daily lives. And they love their creations!

I have attended craft sales where artisans, craftspeople, uncommon men and unique women proudly display their wares, their creations. They made them and they love them!

We cannot help but admire and love what we have had a hand in fashioning.

In the whole universe, in the whole of creation, there is no one exactly like me. And there is no one exactly like you. We are precious in the eyes of our Creator who crafted every atom of our beings and that of every other animate and inanimate object in existence. Each of us is unique. Each of us is one of a kind. Each of us is valued. Each of us is a gift to the world.

As I ponder my own crude creations, I consider the child's rudimentary drawing proudly displayed on the refrigerator. I wonder at the pride of the sculptor in her carving, the carpenter in his cabinet, the craftspeople in their craft shows, the musicians and the authors in their symphonies and anthologies. They all have created something. You and I have created something. We all love our creations.

If we believe in a Creator, would that Creator love us now, and continue to love us in the future, just as any parent loves their child?

We are proudly displayed on God's refrigerator.

Gerald M. Sliva

Chapter 11
Mis-Understanding the Bible

"So pervasive is Mark's eschatology that some scholars regard the entire Gospel as a modified apocalypse, a revelation of unseen realities and a disclosure of events destined soon to climax in God's final intervention in human affairs." — Stephen L. Harris, Understanding the Bible

Unless the reader makes a serious effort, it is easy to misunderstand the Bible. I am a prime example of this fact. Tending to be a lazy reader, I want to understand without any deep thinking, and without referring to a dictionary too often. For example, I invite you to re-read the quotation introducing this chapter. The word *"eschatology"* or some derivative of it appears eleven times within three pages (pages 372 – 374) of the book, *Understanding the Bible*, by Stephen L. Harris where he refers to the Gospel according to Mark. If you understand the meaning of eschatology, you are probably more qualified than I to complete the writing of this book. Trying not to be lazy, I used the on-line Google dictionary and discovered that eschatology is *"the part of theology concerned with death, judgment, and the final destiny of the soul and of humankind."* Weighty stuff, eh? Yep, but we often treat it lightly. Referring to the Bible, Mahatma Gandhi says as much, *"You Christians look after a document containing enough dynamite to blow all civilization to pieces, turn the world upside down and bring peace to a battle-torn planet. But you treat it as though it is nothing more than a piece of literature."*

I profess to be Christian. Gandhi, a non-Christian, is giving Christians a thorough dressing down. Is it really deserved? Do Christians take the Bible for granted? Do I take the Bible for granted? Even though I attend church almost every Sunday, generally attempting attentiveness to the Gospels, Epistles and other readings, I did not read a Bible until later in life. In the 1950's and 1960's the Catholic Church did not enthusiastically recommend Bible reading. I do not recall exactly when I purchased my first Bible. I was probably well over thirty years of age before I took the plunge. Like me, you may have read or heard selected passages from the bible, but have you ever tried reading the whole bible from cover to cover? I tried. Some parts are very inspirational, but some parts, particularly of the Old Testament, can get rather tedious. Edgar J. Goodspeed, in his book *How Came the Bible,* points out that the sixty-six books of the Bible were written over the course of over a thousand years by some forty different authors scattered over two thousand miles from Babylon to Rome. Moreover, since the Bible records the actions, experiences and prophecies of several individuals, it does not follow any chronological pattern, not lending itself to be read from cover to cover.

Interestingly, the Apostle Paul was the first recorder of the New Testament, although he did not know it, nor perhaps, was it his intention at the time. Saul of Tarsus, later called Paul, was initially a fervent persecutor of the followers of Jesus. A devout Jew, Saul believed that it was his duty to snuff out the "heretics" who believed Jesus was the Messiah and had risen from the dead. He thought everyone who followed the way of Jesus Christ should be arrested and possibly face the death penalty as well. However, after his dramatic encounter with the risen Jesus on the road to Damascus, his sudden blindness and the subsequent miraculous regaining of his sight three days later, he became Jesus' most ardent supporter. This occurred in approximately A.D. 35, about two years after Christ's crucifixion. Then, over the course of about thirty years, he travelled some 10,000 miles, preaching to the followers of Jesus, guiding them and encouraging new converts to the religion. Over a period of about seventeen years – from approximately A.D. 50 to A.D. 67, although the exact years are the subject of some debate - he wrote letters of spiritual guidance to the people of seven churches scattered throughout Asia Minor, Greece and Rome: The Romans, the Corinthians, the Galatians, the Ephesians, Philippians, Colossians, and Thessalonians. These letters or epistles, written by Paul between about seventeen to thirty-four years after Jesus' resurrection, were eventually retrieved and assembled as we know them today.

The Gospels of Matthew, Mark, Luke and John were written significantly later, between about A.D. 70 and 90, or about thirty-seven to fifty-seven years after Jesus' death and resurrection. The exact dates of Jesus death and resurrection, as well as the dates of the writing of the New Testament are the subject of some debate; however, the dates cited herein are a very close consensus.

When reading the Bible, I ask myself if I should believe it, *literally,* word for word. Is the bible the inspired Word of God? Or is it the Word of God as selected, and interpreted by man? Or is it man's word, attributed to the mouth of God? Taking as fact every word of the Bible is the subject of much heated debate. For a few moments let's examine some of that debate.

Let's begin with the view of the atheist/cynic/agnostic: The Bible tells a good story, but it is largely legend and myth. Much of the Bible, because it is based on oral tradition, was not written at the time the events occurred. The New Testament was constructed not by Jesus, but by humans recollecting what Jesus said and did. In fact, biblical scholars have ascertained that much of the New Testament was put to paper sixteen to sixty years after the death of Christ. The lag time between experiencing and recording may have led to some distortions of fact. Those of us who have a spouse know that there are often debates and different points of view about events which occurred yesterday or last week, let alone those which occurred twenty or more years ago. Somebody - I accuse my spouse - has a faulty recollection of the facts. Further, scientific studies have shown that eyewitness accounts from a week ago or even from a few hours ago can be faulty and generally unreliable. What about last year, twenty years ago or fifty years ago? How accurate is the human memory?

Most of the Apostles were fishermen. I'm a fisherman too. I've heard stories from other fishermen. They have been known to stretch the facts just a little. Many a fish has continued to grow many years after it has been caught, filleted and consumed. Many a five pounder has grown to be a ten or twelve pounder after the story has been told ad infinitum over the years. I, personally, have never inflated my fish, but I have known others who have done so. What about the Apostles? Being fishermen, were they predisposed to stretching the truth? Can we believe their stories? Jesus wisely failed to recruit lawyers and politicians as His disciples, or the New Testament would be on the scrap heap.

Because of our modern understanding of the world through the sciences such as physics, astronomy, palaeontology and archaeology, we now know some parts of the Bible, particularly the Old Testament, although believed to be accurate when first written, to be incorrect now. Further, superstition, imagination and dreams may have accounted for some biblical stories being documented as visions or signs from God. So, because some parts may be faulty, should we reject the whole document?

Now let's take the view of the faith-filled believer, but one who perhaps does not take every word of the Bible literally. The Bible chronicles man's early understanding of creation, his first interactions with his God and the continuing revelation of God through the old and the new Testaments, so that man's portrait of God evolves through the ages. The Old Testament often depicts God as a dealmaker - you do this for me, and I'll do something for you, a *quid pro quo*. God is sometimes portrayed as a harsh, punitive judge, taking sides in battles, destroying whole cities and inflicting a flood on the entire world. In the New Testament, Jesus more often portrays God as a loving, forgiving Father, as demonstrated in the parable of the Prodigal Son. Furthermore, Jesus' miracles always demonstrate kindness, forgiveness, concern and healing of body and spirit for the sick, the poor and the sinners.

The bible tells a story, written by many people, and interpreted by even more people, about their experiences with Jesus and God. This is a serious subject. It is not likely that the writers, nor the interpreters, have sought to deceive us about the issues of how to live a better life right now or how to improve our afterlife vision. The unceasing interpretation of biblical passages and the controversy of literal versus metaphorical interpretation of the bible can be confusing to us novices. Can this debate eventually lead us to a more mature, loving relationship with our fellow humans, our Creator and all creation?

In his meditations the week of January 6, 2019, Father Richard Rohr covers this topic. He bemoans the absence of love in biblical interpretation. *"For all its inspiration, for all the lives it has changed, the Bible is undeniably problematic. Put in the hands of egocentric, unloving, or power-hungry people or those who have never learned how to read spiritually inspired literature, it is almost always a disaster. History has demonstrated this, century after century, so this is not an unwarranted, disrespectful, or biased conclusion. The burning of heretics, the Crusades, slavery, apartheid, homophobia, and the genocide and oppression of native peoples were all justified through the selective use of Scripture quotes."*

Other religions suffer from a similar malady. Most holy books, like the Bible, are subject to misinterpretation, and in some cases, give contradictory messages. Evil people with their own agendas will take specific quotations, often out of context, using them to justify their heinous acts of violence against the innocent. For example, most Muslims are devout, generous and peace-loving. Yet, certain radicals have hijacked the Muslim faith by their warped interpretation of the Quran.

Many devout believers do not accept every word of the bible literally. In this life, we will never know for sure. We are challenged to remember that when we think we know with certainty, we are likely the most lost. No mortal can know the mind of The Eternal. Perhaps in our afterlife we will get a small glimpse of God's glory, wisdom and the real truth. For that, if it comes at all, we will have to wait. We will have to be patient. However, the theme and the messages presented through the prophets and through Jesus, I take as counsel and guidance for my relationships with God and my neighbour.

For me, the evidence of the essential truth of the New Testament is that almost all the disciples were martyred spreading Jesus' *Good News*. They were fishermen, not scribes. They didn't record every detail of their experiences, but they passed the essence of the information to Matthew, Mark, Luke and John, who were the scribes of the New Testament. The disciples died to spread Jesus' message to all corners of the earth. Not many people willingly, even eagerly, sacrifice their lives for lies and fraud. The disciples died to spread what they knew to be the truth. Today, with the proliferation and dissemination of so many lies, falsehoods and conspiracy theories over the internet, many of us readily accept these obfuscations as facts without investigating their veracity. Yet we find it hard to believe, trust and have faith in the biblical scribes who sought to relay the *Good News*. How many of the authors of internet misinformation would die, as the disciples did, to spread what they believe?

Mahatma Gandhi felt that there was such power in the Bible that it could blow all civilization to pieces, turn the world upside down and bring peace to a battle-torn planet. Studying many religions, Gandhi respected them all. He was a Hindu, not a Christian, but he recognized the strength and inspiration in the words of the Bible. If a non-Christian feels that power, what about us? Was Gandhi prescient with his dynamite metaphor? Perhaps, but maybe the explosion is a slow-motion conflagration rather than a sudden blast. Most of us take for granted the availability and wide distribution of the Bible in English. But that did not occur in an instant. For hundreds of years after Christ's resurrection, the New Testament was available only in the Greek and Hebrew languages, and somewhat later, in Latin.

It was not until the fourteenth century that the Bible was begun to be translated into the vernacular, the common language of the people, first into German; then from 1382 to 1388 into English by John Wycliffe. But Bible translators did not have an easy time of it. Fearing the effects of Bibles being available in the language of lay people, in 1408 the Catholic Church condemned Wycliffe's translation and forbade future translations. Ignoring the Church's hostility toward Bible translations, William Tyndale's English translation of the New Testament was published in 1525. Tyndale's fate was worse than Wycliffe's. In 1536 he was tried for heresy, strangled and burned at the stake. With the advent of the printing press in the mid-fifteenth century and Martin Luther's German translation in 1522 as well as Coverdale's English printing in 1535, the Bible was begun to be more widely available to laity. As of 2017, according to the International Bible Society, the complete Bible has been translated into 670 languages with the complete New Testament being available in 1512 languages. Gossip, bad news and lies travel fast and are believed immediately. The *Good News* of the Bible takes time to work its miracles.

"So, Mahatma," that's me talking to Gandhi. "The fuse has been lit. The explosion is forthcoming."

The Bible, particularly the New Testament, in my estimation, is not just a piece of literature.

For certain?

I know not.

Yet, I have faith!

Not sure of the size of my faith. It might be small! According to Matthew 17:20, Jesus said, "I tell you solemnly, if your faith were the size of a mustard seed you could say to this mountain, 'Move from here to there,' and it would move; nothing would be impossible for you."

Do I believe I'll be moving mountains anytime soon?

Chapter 12
Space Invaders

God created little green men and little green women. They come from other planets. And they have visited earth. - Fact, alternative fact or fake news?

Being intrigued by the possibility of space aliens and flying saucers, during the 1960's and 1970's, science fiction was my preferred reading genre. One November evening in 1968 when I was driving on Highway # 11 south of Saskatoon, Saskatchewan, I encountered what I can only describe as a UFO - an orange, glowing, saucer-shaped object travelling slowly across the horizon, about one-half mile from our vehicle. Ever curious, I turned off the main road to try to get closer to the object. However, it had sunk below the tree line and even as I drove around the area, I never spotted it again. I will never know whether I was close to having a close encounter, or whether I saw some other unexplained phenomenon. It matters not. What I now know is that many of the devices envisioned by science fiction writers long before they were invented have now become fact: space travel, solar power, artificial intelligence, organ transplants and much, much more. Perhaps intelligent creatures from other planets are another possibility.

God has created a limitless universe, impossible for the human mind to comprehend. But that won't stop us from trying. Science and astronomy, through our novice piercings of space by NASA and the Hubble telescope, are providing us with elementary ideas of a universe incomprehensible to the human mind. It is unending, infinite and eternal as is its Creator. Every day we learn more about the absolute miracles of creation, but we can never know it all. Humans have tried to bend their minds enough to understand that one could travel through space for millions and billions of years forever searching for the edge of existence, and never find it. There is no end, no barrier, no brick wall and no sign with the cryptic announcement, *"You have reached the edge of the universe. There is nothing on the other side of this wall."* (On second thought, maybe God created a brick wall out there in the nether regions just to keep humans out. I just don't know.)

Early humans pondered the earth, the sea and the sky and all its creatures, vainly imagining that this was all created exclusively for man's use, pleasure or plunder. We think Earth is the centre of all creation and the universe is created for us. We ought to think again.

We now know that earth is the equivalent of a particle of dust in unending space. Did God create the limitless universe only for proud, deceitful, polluting, ungrateful humans on this speck of a planet we call earth? Or did God plan the evolution of other sentient beings on other distant planets, beings perhaps much more humane, forming a society perhaps much more willing to "love God with their whole body, mind and spirit; and to love their neighbour as themselves"? And if human-like aliens exist on other planets, is it likely they would have religions? Would they have a *Golden Rule* equivalent?

Questions of UFO's, extra-terrestrials, humanoids from other planets as well as messages from the far reaches of the universe have been the subject of much science fiction, astronomy, investigative science, and UFO'ology.

The all-powerful, loving force we know as God provides limitless human life in God's own image and likeness. In North America we believe we know God's image and likeness. What is God's image and likeness? We believe God is exactly like us, not like our neighbour with a different culture, religion, sexual orientation or skin colour. There is an excellent chance that we are wrong, that God is much larger, more magnanimous and infinitely more creative than we might envision. On distant planets there could be other humans/humanoids, perhaps much more advanced than we. Perhaps they have blue tinged flesh and superhuman powers as in the 2009 movie "Avatar". Or maybe they are diminutive, green fleshed humanoids communicating electromagnetically. Or they might be very similar to us – varied in culture, language, skin colour and stature. All creation reflects God's love, image and likeness, and is likely much more marvellous and expansive than we can ever imagine. If we ever make it to the place we call heaven, we may be able to open our eyes to appreciate the wonders God has created.

If there really are human-like beings on other planets, can we expect to see them on earth? Not likely. Scientists and astronomers tell us it is nearly impossible to travel the distances from even the closest habitable planet to our home on earth unless a super-intelligent race has evolved and solved the mystery of time travel, travel at the speed of light or developed teleportation, permitting them to travel instantaneously across great distances. If aliens actually do visit earth, they might have to use a method similar to that employed in the popular science fiction series, *Star Trek*. "Beam me up Scotty", would be their mantra. As remote a possibility as that might be, even if an advanced civilization of extra-terrestrial beings visited earth, we would never know it. If they had such superior intellect, knowledge and technology to reach earth, they would have the wisdom not to reveal themselves. Just a cursory observation of our world would quickly demonstrate to them that we would fear them, go to war with them (shades of Donald Trump's *Space Force*), or build a wall to keep them out. Think about how we humans treat anyone different from ourselves. Fear, suspicion and aggression! If space aliens come to our planet is there any chance we would treat them any better than we treat anyone else who is different from us? Very few of us are open-minded enough to welcome all strangers, aliens, or anyone who is different. Until and unless humanity changes it is unlikely that we will encounter creatures from other worlds.

On the other hand, they could visit us and be even more aggressive warmongers than we humans. Others, more intelligent than I, have concerns with possible space creatures. If they exist, invade our planet and turn out to be far more advanced than we are, we could be on the receiving end of slavery, first-hand. In the 2004 National

Geographic Channel presentation *Naked Science: Alien Contact*, Stephen Hawking is rather gloomy about extra-terrestrials visiting us. He says, "I think it would be a disaster. The extra-terrestrials would probably be far in advance of us. The history of advanced races meeting more primitive people on this planet is not very happy, and they were the same species. I think we should keep our heads low."

Intelligent beings in remote, distant reaches of the universe? Or maybe in our neighbourhood? Who knows? Jesus has given us the answer in Matthew 19:26, "For God, everything is possible".

Part 3 – Faith and Fraud

*"We have met the enemy and he is us." –
Pogo, by Walt Kelly*

Chapter 13
True Belief – Faith

"The fundamental cause of the trouble is that in the modern world the stupid are cocksure while the intelligent are full of doubt." — Bertrand Russell

True belief and certainty are very easy. Especially when it involves a scandal, a rumour or some real evil regarding someone who is not part of our clan, religion, political persuasion, sexual orientation or colour. On the other hand, no amount of preaching, Bible study, pulpit pounding evangelism, promises of paradise or threats of eternal damnation will convince one of the existence of God, whose existence must be felt within our hearts.

God began the creation of the universe billions of years ago. (Some Biblical literalists say it happened only 6,000 to 13,000 years ago.) Jesus rose two thousand years ago. Those are distant events. Maybe we will be forgiven if we have some questions, a few lingering doubts about the authenticity of creation and of Jesus' resurrection. The holocaust occurred about eighty years ago, and there are holocaust deniers. The Newtown Massacre at Sandy Hook Elementary School happened only six years ago and there are conspiracy theorists purporting that the massacre was a hoax, all staged by professional actors. The horrific shootings at the Tree of Life Congregation Synagogue in Pittsburgh took place on Saturday, October 27, 2018, and just four days later there were already reports that white nationalists are spreading rumours of the massacre being a hoax. By the time you read these words, there will be fresh events, maybe more spectacular, horrific or memorable than the aforementioned. And there will be new doubters and deniers.

If we have trouble believing incidents which happened just recently, God and Jesus have some work to do convincing the sceptics about events surrounding Jesus' miracles, torture and crucifixion which occurred some two thousand years ago as well as God's creations beginning billions of years ago or, perhaps an eternity ago. Or rather, maybe we, the sceptics, have some work to do examining the evidence.

Faith does not come easy. But we ought not to despair if we have doubts. Paul Tillich (1886-1965), author and theologian says, "Doubt isn't the opposite of faith; it is an element of faith." We are all on a continuum somewhere between absolute belief and trust (theism) versus absolute disbelief and rejection (atheism). Many of us are somewhere in the middle (agnostic) but leaning toward either belief or doubt. Humans, endowed with God-given intelligence, want proof to back up their faith. My guess is that for the vast majority of us, absolute proof of God's existence or Jesus' resurrection will not be forthcoming – at least not in this life. We'll have to die to find out for certain. At that point, faith will not be required. George Carlin wisecracked about the theist's beliefs: "Tell people there's an invisible man in the sky who created the universe, and the vast majority will believe you. Tell them the paint is wet, and they have to touch it to be sure."

"Well, George," - That's me talking to George Carlin. - "You died back in 2008; so, by now you may have had an opportunity to touch the *Paint*."

There will always be doubters and deniers. Jesus told us as much in the parable of the rich man and Lazarus (Luke 16:30-31) where Abraham says that some people will persist in their cynicism even in the face of undeniable evidence:

"'Ah no, father Abraham,' said the rich man, 'but if someone comes to them from the dead, they will repent.'

"He (Abraham) said to him, 'If they will not listen either to Moses or to the Prophets, they will not be convinced even if someone should rise from the dead.'"

We all want proof. Even saints had their doubts. Mother Teresa of Calcutta was tormented with uncertainty, writing, *"Please pray especially for me that I may not spoil His work and that Our Lord may show Himself — for there is such terrible darkness within me, as if everything was dead."*

We are all in the same boat, on stormy seas. We want the Lord to show himself. Even the apostles, who knew Jesus personally, questioned their faith. We've all heard of "Doubting Thomas" who refused to believe Jesus had risen from the dead unless, according to scripture, he could touch the wounds of the resurrected Jesus. Jesus knew that unquestioning faith is not easy. He said to Thomas and the others there present, *"You believe because you can see me.*

Happy are those who have not seen, and yet believe." (John 20:29) Most of us, even faith-filled believers, have more than once said, "God, please give me a sign – a lottery win would help - even just a little sign to show me that you are with me, that you exist, that you are real. If you do that, I will truly believe." We are not alone in our misgivings. Even Jesus on the cross, according to the Bible, despondently cried, "My God! My God! Why have you abandoned me?"

It seems, for humans, it is easier, without a shred of real evidence, to believe rumours, falsehoods and conspiracy theories about an individual or a group, than to believe the *Good News* of the New Testament. Jesus could come back and live again, perform his miracles for body and soul, die again and rise again in a new location every year. It would be to no avail. For many of us, even if we saw it with our own eyes, it would be labelled as a hoax, trickery, witchcraft or fake news.

On his arm, Anthony Bourdain had tattooed, "I am certain of nothing." However, there are those who are certain of the existence of God, of the resurrected Jesus and of an amazing life after we die. Some of those who were certain were Jesus, the apostles, Matthew, Mark, Luke and John as well as St Paul who was once a persecutor of Christians. As we search for evidence and absolute proof of God's existence and Jesus' resurrection, we might be wise to reflect upon the words of Thomas Aquinas: "To one who has faith, no explanation is necessary. To one without faith, no explanation is possible."

Chapter 14
Common Ground

Those who do not know God, yet love their neighbour, are halfway up the ladder to heaven; whereas, those who profess to love God while being indifferent or antagonistic to the plight of their neighbour have yet to step on the lowest rung.

Is there a universal truth, a common ground for all religions and for all people? Have humans, and maybe even animals, been endowed with a built-in guidance system programmed to love, sympathize, empathize with and to help and comfort those in need? Many religions profess exclusive rights to kinship with the Eternal and the keys to the brotherhood of man. And some radicals have even perverted us such that some of us view all religions other than our own as unworthy. Is there a chance that we all (believers in all religions, agnostics and atheists) know what God and our neighbour want and need of us, but which we are slow to deliver? Do we all share common ground in some expression of *The Golden Rule*? A study of the world's major religions seems to say so, each in their own way:

Christianity - "So in everything, do to others what you would have them do to you, for this sums up the Law and the Prophets." Matthew 7:12 NIV

Taoism - "Regard your neighbour's gain as your gain, and your neighbour's loss as your own loss." Tai Shang Kan Yin P'ien

Islam - "None of you truly believes until he wishes for his brother what he wishes for himself." Number 13 of Imam "Al-Nawawi's Forty Hadiths."

Hinduism - "This is the sum of duty: do not do to others what would cause pain if done to you." Mahabharata 5:1517

Buddhism- "Hurt not others in ways that you yourself would find hurtful." Udana-Varga 5:18

Native American Spirituality - "All things are our relatives; what we do to everything, we do to ourselves. All is really One." Black Elk

Judaism - "...thou shalt love thy neighbor as thyself.", Hebrew Scriptures (a.k.a. Old Testament) Leviticus 19:18

A look at Zoroastrianism, Sikhism, Unitarianism, Shintoism, Jainism, Confucianism, Brahmanism and Baha'i Faith all reveal similar entreaties. Richard Dawkins, avowed atheist, in his series *Sex, Death and the Meaning of Life* states that atheists, too, have a moral code which could be paraphrased as "treat others as you wish to be treated".

The *Golden Rule* is synonymous with nonviolence as evidenced by the lives and the statements of three people who dedicated their lives to love:

Martin Luther King, Jr: "All humanity is involved in a simple process, and all men are brothers. To the degree that I harm my brother, no matter what he is doing to me, to that extent I am harming myself."

Mahatma Gandhi: "Joy comes not out of the infliction of pain upon others but out of pain voluntarily borne by oneself."

Jesus: "You must love your neighbor as yourself." Mark 12:31

In his book, *Perspective, The Golden Rule*, David Meakes time and again stresses the importance of morality and family values promoting the *Golden Rule* in action. Further, he advocates that worldwide educational curricula supplement familial values by including *Golden Rule* knowledge and practice throughout all educational systems. Does all humanity want to express *The Golden Rule* in some fashion? Do we want to live it, but we find living it much more difficult than stating it? Perhaps this is reflected in how the Wizard of Id cynically and satirically views how Western society has twisted the *Golden Rule*: "**Remember the Golden Rule! Whoever has the gold, makes the rules!**"

Chapter 15
Finding Jesus

Who is having the more spiritual experience, the guy sitting in church thinking about fishing or the guy out fishing thinking about God?

From the dawn of man's existence, he has known there is more to life than the three score and ten years we wander on this earth. There is ample archaeological evidence that prehistoric humans, searching for deities, came to worship fire. Not surprising! The fires in the sky: the sun, the moon, the stars and the planets were mysterious and worthy of worship. Then when man learned how to harness fire, using it for light, warmth, cooking and a variety of alchemy tasks, he became intrigued at the possibility of controlling his god. Making animal and even human sacrifices, often as burnt offerings, was seen as a way to appease, worship and control their god(s). The practise even carried over into monotheism in the Old Testament where there are numerous references to sacrificing and burning/roasting animals to appease God. The First Nations peoples of North America worshipped the Great Spirit. Before them, Druids, Egyptians, Incas, Greeks and Romans all had some concepts of an afterlife, a Creator or creators. Man knows that he is not alone, that someone greater than he propelled the universe, the wheel of life, into motion and nourishes its growth. Upon becoming a sentient being, realizing that the Loving Force, the Creator of all things existed, man longed for and searched for his Maker. Then when man believed that he had found that Loving Force, in an effort to become closer, to develop a relationship with his God, he wondered, praised and worshipped. Did this happen in an instant, in an Adam and Eve? Or did it evolve? If man evolved, as we have been led to believe, at what stage did man know enough about his God to be worthy of eternal life? Or is all life eternal?

Though not many of us would openly admit it, we are all searching for knowledge of the future, the meaning of life, something more permanent than our earthly existence. Some will do it in church. Others try on the golf course or in a fishing boat. We are searching for God, Allah, Jesus, Yahweh, Krishna, Buddha, some eternal loving force. When we think we can't find them, or when we may have searched in the wrong places, we imagine or invent what we regard as reasonable facsimiles or substitutions. Examples abound of gullible people paying ridiculous sums via eBay for food items that "kinda look" like Jesus. One person found a Jesus image in a pierogi and sold it for $1775; another person netted $28,000 for a grilled cheese sandwich purported to have an image of the Virgin Mary. A quick Google search will reveal many more examples. To quote Michel De Montaigne, Essays, "*Man is certainly crazy. He could not make a mite, and he makes gods by the dozen.*"

Jesus said something about no man being able to serve two masters. We devote the most time and attention to whatever or whomever we want to serve. For many of us in the twenty-first century, it is addiction to the smartphone – yes, it is an addiction, perhaps more dangerous than smoking, alcohol or drugs, simply because it is so pervasive - where people meet God unintentionally and tragically by texting while driving. But there are many other places we can "*pray*". The daily horoscope, soothsayers and fortune tellers are good places to start the search for what we believe are answers to the meaning of life and the future. Or if we still haven't found our guru, we can worship our athletes. Many of us have changed religions or given up on worship entirely, but we still worship at the altars of baseball, football, basketball or hockey, forever faithful to the same team or the same athlete: Tiger Woods, Magic Johnson or Peyton Manning. And we can worship our politicians, particularly if they lower our taxes, because that's our money anyhow. We worship them even if they lower taxes to take programs and funding away from the poor, disabled, veterans, widows, orphans and refugees. What would Jesus think of that? I've seen people on television comparing some politicians to Jesus Christ. How's that for worship? Then when we can't find an athlete or politician to worship, we invent and fawn upon imaginary superheroes like Antman, Superman, Spiderman or Batman, believing that they are saviours. Still another alternative is magic. Not finding God in the marvels of humanity and the mysteries of nature, His creation, we want to be mystified by the unknown, by magic. We wonder at, idolize and adore David Blaine, Chris Angel and David Copperfield. Then, if we still haven't found Jesus we might turn to celebrities, movie stars and reality television personalities to pay homage to. Finally, if none of the above satisfy our longings, we can try to find security in worshipping the almighty dollar by maxing out our credit cards and accumulating goods we think we need, or alternatively piling money into gold, stock portfolios, IRA's, RRSP's, real estate investments and a myriad other "false gods".

I'm guilty! Much of our Western society is, too.

Sometimes we don't have to search for Jesus. He often comes to our doorstep. Our doorbell rings and there are two impeccably dressed young men from the Church of Jesus Christ of Latter-Day Saints, commonly known as Mormons, inviting us to learn more about their brand of religion. Or we might be lucky enough to open the door and find an elderly couple holding up a recent edition of *Watchtower* magazine, the periodic publication of the Jehovah's Witnesses. I have yet to meet many who invite either group in to learn more. But the proselytizers must get a few bites. It's probably a lot like fishing – if no fish bite, you eventually give up. I don't see them giving up.

On one occasion, many years ago, being curious about why the Jehovah's Witnesses prohibit blood transfusions, I accepted an edition of *Watchtower* containing an article explaining the reason for the blood transfusion ban. The jw.org website contains the following explanation: "Both the Old and New Testaments clearly command us to abstain from blood. (Genesis 9:4; Leviticus 17:10; Deuteronomy 12:23; Acts 15:28, 29) Also, God views blood as representing life. (Leviticus 17:14) So we avoid taking blood not only in obedience to God but also out of respect for him as the Giver of life." In the chapter entitled *Mis-Understanding the Bible* I already commented on bible interpretation and the wisdom, or lack of it, of reacting to every word of the bible.

For some, the traditional religions have not been helpful in finding God, so there is a proliferation of new religions, all promising to show the way to Jesus, God, Heaven or the promised land.

So, back to our question, "Who is having the more spiritual experience, the guy sitting in church thinking about fishing or the guy out fishing thinking about God?" The answer, of course, is a no brainer. Jesus loves fishermen. He chose many to be his disciples. This leads me to propose starting a vibrant new religion: The Living Waters Fishing Boathouse Church where angling enthusiasts can fish, think about God and experience God's Great Outdoors while listening to inspirational gospel music ("Shall We Gather By the River", "Wade in the Water" and other old-time water-themed favourites), selected New Testament readings and an animated five minute sermon followed by a delicious shore lunch. Call me crazy if you wish, but in some countries starting a new religion is, to coin a phrase, "as easy as shooting fish in a barrel".

Huffington Post points out that the IRS in the USA, to respect religious liberties outlined in the American Constitution, makes the rules surrounding churches and religious organizations intentionally vague. That can lead to some very shady and questionable practices on the part of some churches and ministers. Comedian and satirist John Oliver proved as much in an episode of his HBO show,

"Last Week Tonight", where he skewers several bible punching televangelists for their preying – maybe they confused the word "praying" with "preying" - on gullible and desperate followers. To further make his point, John Oliver started his very own tax-exempt church and declared himself "megareverend". The episode was posted to YouTube August 16, 2015. A YouTube search for "Televangelists: Last Week Tonight with John Oliver" will yield results on your computer to view the scandalous 20-minute episode. God will have to be very forgiving or there will be a special Hell for religious leaders who betray the trust of their followers.

According to *Adherents*, an independent, non-religiously affiliated organization which tracks and monitors religions, there are approximately 4300 different religions in the world, the eight largest (and their number of believers) being as follows:

Christianity (2.1 billion)
Islam (1.3 billion)
Nonreligious (Secular/Agnostic/Atheist) (1.1 billion)
Hinduism (900 million)
Chinese traditional religion (394 million)
Buddhism (376 million)
Primal-indigenous (300 million)
African traditional and Diasporic (100 million)

This list has some intriguing components, classifying the non-religious and neo-pagans as religious groups. Also, interestingly, in my research I discovered that there are some 41,000 different Christian denominations, with almost half of all Christians professing to be Roman Catholic.

Then, even within the Roman Catholic Church there are seven different rites, or religious traditions, all under the umbrella of the Pope in Rome. The most common rite in North America is the Latin Rite where, until 1965, the Mass was celebrated in the Latin language. Many Latin Catholics believe they are Roman Catholics as opposed to Greek or Ukrainian Catholics when, in fact, they are all Roman Catholics. The Greek and Ukrainian Catholics follow the Byzantine rituals but are still loyal to the Pope in Rome; thus, they are "Roman Catholics". The seven Roman Catholic Rites are Latin, Byzantine, Alexandrian, Syriac, Armenian, Maronite, and Chaldean. Further, there are different cultures, traditions and practices within each of these rites. Not professing to be a theologian or biblical scholar, I will not attempt to explain or differentiate. For readers interested in studying this further, there is a wealth of information on the internet. As well, Father Richard Rohr, whose meditations I read daily, covers many aspects of Catholicism, Protestantism, Islamism, Hinduism and Buddhism. Finding value in all religions, he examines their traditions and practices in a scholarly, caring manner.

Christianity and Islam cover the religious affiliation of more than half of the world's population and are the two religions most widely spread across the world. If all non-religious people formed a single religion, it would be the world's third largest. Finally, for trivia buffs, nearly 75 per cent of the world's population practises one of the five most influential religions of the world: Buddhism, Christianity, Hinduism, Islam, and Judaism.

Humanity continues to search for a universal truth, something eternal and unifying. But with over seven billion individuals on our planet, it is virtually impossible to find two people with identical theologies. This leads me to conclude that either there are a plethora of visions of God, our origins and creationism/evolution; that humans are truly searching for our Source, our Loving Force, our Creator and the meaning of life; or people are looking for their own special tax dodge. It seems to me that if a group does not ascribe to the *Golden Rule*, it should not be permitted the tax breaks afforded religions.

After watching John Oliver's HBO clip and researching on-line material, I conclude that any sincere (or even insincere) group of individuals searching for God can concoct their own religion in Canada or the United States of America. Fraudsters and scam artists have the same opportunity. Is it too easy to start a new religion?

Are not 4300 different religions sufficient enough from which to choose? But, just in case, perhaps one more should be started. Maybe it's my turn. I see a huge untapped opportunity in vacant anchor stores in local shopping malls. The heyday is over for shopping malls. They are on the decline. The internet is killing them. Because of Amazon and on-line shopping, big box stores in shopping malls around the world are suffering from falling sales and bankruptcies. Once thriving Sears is now a vacant hulk in the local mall. I'm here to help. I promise to bring a *revival* – pun intended – to the malls. Not everyone is a fishing enthusiast; therefore, some folks will not join my Living Waters Fishing Boathouse Church. People need choices. Some will prefer to "Shop 'n Pray" at my Sacred Sears Miracle Church where there is the promise of short sermons, huge miracles, daily specials and cash collections hourly. I know the congregation will be generous to help fund a private jet to whisk me around the world to spread the Sacred Sears word.

With each religion, sect or cult preaching that it has the only path to eternal bliss, finding God or finding Jesus sometimes seems like a confusing task. One old story about "finding Jesus" demonstrates this.

One beautiful summer morning a Christian congregation gathers by the river to conduct several baptisms. Unbeknownst to them, they awaken an aging, derelict alcoholic who has been under a nearby bridge sleeping off the results of his previous night's celebrations. Still in his half-drunken stupor, the unshaven, scruffy gentleman stumbles into the assembly of believers.

The minister conducting the baptisms, seizing the opportunity to bring one more soul to salvation, invites the intruder to come forward.

"Do you want to find Jesus?" the minister asks the dishevelled fellow.

Dazed, somewhat taken aback by the invitation, and not wanting to seem uncooperative, the derelict mumbles, "Sure. Why not?!" And he wades into the river beside the minister who promptly plunges him headfirst into the water, holding him submerged for a few seconds, then lifting his head above water and asking him, "Have you found Jesus?"

The bewildered alcoholic, coughing and sputtering, mutters, "No, I haven't."

Plunging him in once more, the minister holds him under a little longer, finally drags him out and asks again, "Have you found Jesus yet?"

"No, not yet," the inebriated fellow answers.

The minister, with his eyes raised toward heaven, repeats the whole ceremony one more time, praying for a more positive result. This time, when he finally pulls his recruit out of the water, he insists, "Well, *now* have you found Jesus?"

The old alcoholic, getting tired of the repeated plunges finally retorts, "No, I haven't. Are you sure this is where he fell in?"

As I see it, with all the different religions, sects within religions and the abundance of Christian divisions we have somehow lost our way. Rather than looking for what makes us brothers and sisters with One Father in heaven, each group isolates itself by setting man-made boundaries, rules, precepts and practices. (We all want to belong to the winning team. We just cannot seem to believe that the whole human race is on one team.) Then each group says, if you do these things you belong, and you will go to heaven, or at least you have a reasonable shot at it. However, if you don't believe exactly what we believe and practise exactly what we practise, you are an outsider. You don't belong, and don't fit in. In fact, you might just go to hell.

Worship and praise! Beautiful stuff which brings us closer to our God! If it does, should it not also bring humanity closer together, unite us as the human race, as brothers and sisters, sons and daughters of our Creator? Where did we go wrong? Why do we have Muslims, Christians and Jews, all worshipping the same God, at odds with one another? Why do we have 41,000 different Christian groups all forming their own styles of worship, their own religious practices, all claiming to know the truth? I sometimes wonder about the emphasis of church leaders on differences in dogma and ritual rather than a focus on our common belief in one God of all and the *Golden Rule*. Could that be one reason humanity has such difficulty achieving peace and spiritual harmony?

In his meditation of January 27, 2020, Father Richard Rohr gives us a similar message, *"It is amazing how religion has turned the biblical idea of faith around 180 degrees – into a need and even a right to certain knowing, complete predictability, and perfect assurance about whom and what God likes and doesn't like. Why do we think we can have the Infinite Mystery of God in our quite finite pocket? We supposedly know what God is going to say or do next, because we think our particular denomination has it all figured out."*

Do I believe that the God who created us and the whole universe has time for our petty religious politics? Or do I believe that God wants LOVE in whatever form we can give it? Do I believe that Jesus wants everyone to be part of his family, and God to be our Father (or our Mother)? Seems straightforward and simple enough – Jesus said it: love God; love your neighbour.

Chapter 16
Church, Faith, Fraud

"On the most elementary level, you do not have to go to church to be a Christian. You do not have to go home to be married either. But in both cases if you do not, you will have a very poor relationship." - R. Kent Hughes

R. Kent Hughes is not here to defend his statement, but I am here to refute at least part of it. The contention that I do not have to go home to be married is true; moreover, if I do not go home it is almost impossible for me to have a meaningful relationship with my spouse. However, I dispute the false equivalency he makes regarding going to church. Church attendance is not necessary for a relationship with God or with Jesus any more than attendance at a casino is necessary for one to develop a relationship with a gambling habit. There are, and always have been other methods of developing relationships, either with God or with gambling.

People have all kinds of reasons for not going to church, but the one we hear most often is that church is irrelevant; the leaders are hypocritical and even immoral. It is true that there have been numerous high-profile scandals and atrocities in churches. There is no shortage of examples:

August 2018: The revelation of the abuse of over 1000 children by over 300 Catholic priests in Philadelphia. Further, there are allegations that church leaders knew about the crimes and took little or no remedial action.

May 7, 2019: A *Christian Post* headline, "After 40 years 'Megachurch' pastor slams Christianity and quits, deacon claims he had affair". Dave Gass, the former pastor of Grace Family Fellowship of Pleasant Hill, Missouri, made this announcement: "After 40 years of being a devout follower, 20 of those being an evangelical pastor, I am walking away from faith."

August 2018: A pastor of 19 years for a Winnipeg church has resigned after being criminally charged in the State of California with attempting to arrange a sexual act with a minor.

Over the years there have been numerous high-profile church and cult leaders involved in various scandals including fraud, sexual misconduct and worse. The list includes Warren Jeffs, Ted Haggard and Jimmy Swaggart. A quick Google search will reveal many more.

I avoid wasting my time watching the huckster and flimflam televangelists. But in the late 1970's, while television channel surfing, I chanced upon a couple of bad acting bible punchers promoting their Christian-themed park, Heritage USA. Their whole demeanour was hilarious. Yet the PTL (Praise the Lord) Club of baby-faced Jim

Bakker and his crocodile tear streaked, mascara-laden wife Tammy Faye talked gullible supporters out of millions of dollars. Not surprisingly, the Bakker's religious empire was rocked by scandal when it was revealed that Jim Bakker used proceeds from their TV shows and their theme park to make secret payments to a secretary as hush money in an attempt to cover up a sexual encounter. The secretary, Jessica Hahn, later accused Bakker of rape. The upshot of the whole mess was that baby-faced Jimmy was sentenced to 45 years in prison relating to charges of mail and wire fraud conspiracy.

Hearing of the demise of the Bakkers, I paid no attention to them for many years, except that I had heard that Tammy Faye died of cancer in 2007. Then in the summer of 2009, while on vacation in Branson, Missouri, once again channel surfing, I was shocked to see Jim Bakker - it turns out that preacher Bakker was paroled in 1994 after spending only five years behind bars - once again brazenly begging for money to "rebuild the Holy Land". (Pardon my cynicism, but I wonder how many donations actually reached the Holy Land.) He began broadcasting his *Jim Bakker Show* from Branson in 2003. There he peddles his brand of apocalypse forecasting, end-times, fear-based Christianity where he sells fuel-less generators, doomsday guidebooks and freeze-dried food with a shelf-life of up to 30 years.

Jim Bakker's show is just one instance of how the emphasis on dogma, hype or showmanship by many television evangelical hucksters discourages critical thinking and reasoning, thereby providing fraud and scam artists opportunities to mislead gullible devoted followers willing to open their wallets to support any hare-brained scheme promoted by would-be "Christian" preachers. Fraud, sexual impropriety and misuse of funds are bad enough. But the most egregious crimes are perpetrated by fanatics and cult leaders who brainwash their followers into committing heinous acts under the guise of religion. Some of the most infamous and tragic ones follow:

Charles Manson (1934-2017) terrorized frightened Americans in the late 1960s, convincing his followers to commit vicious murders in his name.

In November 1978 the deranged Reverend Jim Jones (1931-1978), leader of the People's Temple, in Jonestown, Guyana instructed all members to commit suicide by drinking poisoned punch. On that day 918 people died, nearly a third of whom were children.

In April 1993 in Waco, Texas, cult leader David Koresh (1959-1993) of the Branch Davidians resisted the FBI and other federal law enforcement authorities for 51 days. The result was the tragic death of over 75 men, women and children.

These few examples are all factual. A quick internet search will reveal dozens more. But are they good reasons, or merely my excuse for not spending time in worship? Churches are run by human beings who are prone to temptation, error, mismanagement, mental illness and lust for power. Cult leaders, priests, ministers, bishops, church leaders, and even popes are all subject to human frailties. They are like every other human being on the planet. The sad fact is that very few church leaders make headlines for the good works they perform even if they far outnumber those who fail in their calling. High profile Mother Teresa's are a rare breed; there are many more who do good works quietly, and unnoticed, far away from the glare of publicity.

Not going to church because there are some, albeit a small percentage, of misguided or evil church leaders would be like not going to visit a medical doctor because some doctors, albeit a small percentage, are lazy, incompetent, sexually predatory, or unprofessional. But the offenders must be rooted out, prevented from practising and, if appropriate, be charged with their crimes. If I encounter or hear of one of these, I will not ascribe it to all doctors or all religious. Most doctors, medical specialists, preachers, priests and church leaders are sincere, loving and professional humans. By avoiding them or not heeding their counsel, I may be missing valuable life and death information.

Church is boring! If that is truly the case, perhaps I am not attending a church which inspires, teaches and supports the ideals of Christianity, Islamism, Judaism or the true values of the *Golden Rule*. Or maybe I have the wrong attitude. If my church does not help me to be a better person, maybe I expect to be served rather than to serve. The famous words of John F. Kennedy come to mind "Ask not what your country can do for you; ask what you can do for your country."

Coming back to Mr R. Kent Hughes' statement, "On the most elementary level, you do not have to go to church to be a Christian. You do not have to go home to be married either. But in both cases if you do not, you will have a very poor relationship." In my view, there are many methods of developing a relationship. The first criterion for developing it is to *want it*. I can spout all I want about wanting a relationship with my Creator or my Saviour, but if I take no steps in that direction, I am as hypocritical as the church leaders involved in well-publicized scandals. If I am hooked on gambling, I can do it without the casino. I can lose my money just as efficiently by buying lottery tickets, betting on sports and frequenting the horse races as well as pouring cash into the slots at the casino. Likewise, if I am truly hooked on Jesus, I may be able to get my fix more efficiently by praying, studying the Bible, performing charitable works and being in awe of creation as well as participating in the church of my choice. Will my idea of the *right* church make it easier?

"One hundred religious persons knit into unity by careful organization do not constitute a church any more than eleven dead men make a football team" - A.W. Tozer

We will each make our own choices as to how to enrich the relationships we value. To set the record straight, despite the failings of many religious bureaucrats, I attend the church of my choice. By participating in the liturgy, hymns and prayers, I feel spiritually refreshed. By meditating on the words of the scriptures, I am reminded of the many ways in which I am loved. Engaging in critical thinking, assessing the words and the actions of our religious leaders, as well as active participation in worship is my choice. I believe church attendance helps me to develop a better relationship with the Loving Force we call God and my fellow human beings. I also believe that church attendance guarantees nothing. Without a sincere effort on my part, I will never develop the relationships I seek, or internalize and live the *Golden Rule*.

Part 4 – Religious Politi-Sex

"When authorities warn you of the sinfulness of sex, there is an important lesson to be learned. Do not have sex with the authorities."
– Matt Groening

Chapter 17
Bathroom Debacle

"It's not easy being green." - Joe Raposo via Kermit the Frog

It's not easy being green, or black, or disabled, or gay or what might be perceived as different in any way. Minorities around the world have never had an easy time of it. Neither is it easy being an individual with what the masses characterize as a deviant sexual orientation. In small town Kuroki in the 1950's, there was little serious discussion of homosexuality or, for that matter, any other kind of sexuality. I recall one older gentleman whom everyone *knew* was homosexual, but to my knowledge, he was accepted as a human being. In Canada in the mid-twentieth century and earlier, homosexual activity, even between consenting adults, was against the law. One day while reading the newspaper – children did that back in the '50's – remember, there were no home computers or smart phones and we didn't yet have a television – I discovered an article about the RCMP raiding a bathhouse in Toronto, rounding up dozens of homosexual men, and charging them with illegal acts. Leaving sexual activity out of it, during the 1950's and 1960's a "fruit machine" project by the Government of Canada was a concerted campaign to eliminate all homosexuals from the civil service, the Royal Canadian Mounted Police (RCMP), and the military. The project lost its funding in the 1960's, but not before a substantial number of people lost their jobs and the RCMP had collected files on over 9,000 homosexual "suspects".

The mania to root out homosexuals subsided somewhat when same-sex activity was decriminalized in Canada with the passing of Bill C-150 in 1969. During debate over that piece of legislation, Pierre Elliott Trudeau, then Attorney General and Justice Minister, famously commented, "There is no place for the state in the bedrooms of the nation."

Seems as though, in some quarters, the state now wants a place in the bathrooms of the nation. A segment of our society continually gets its knickers in a twist about homosexuals, transsexuals, bisexuals and queers. These non-heterosexuals are expected to clearly identify their sexuality and always use the appropriate bathroom. Who thought the task of going to the bathroom was going to get this complicated? When I have to go to the bathroom, my bowels and bladder won't wait for someone to examine my genitals to ensure I do my business in the politically correct time and place. If I got to go, then *I HAVE TO GO!* As I age, life takes on a new urgency, particularly if I need to find a bathroom. The bladder has its own momentum, which *Depends* – pun intended - on one's age. I don't need urination aggravation.

It seems that some politicians, with nothing better to do than talk about urination legislation and foul bowel movements, want to legislate where and when defecation and urination events might legally occur. Sometimes I can't wait! Speaking specifically for myself and more generally for all seniors I ask, "Do you want me to do my business in my pants?"

I know, I know. The politicians aren't picking on seniors. They are picking on transgender folks, whom some politicians contend must defecate and urinate in designated places according to *someone's* determination of their sex. I wonder who that *someone* might be. Will there be a new occupation, a new job description, *someone* who specializes in determining which bathroom I must use? (Perhaps politicians are carrying job creation a little too far.) Or will the designated private parts inspector be a generalist, one-minute flipping burgers at McDonald's and the next minute checking a customer's pubis to determine which bathroom they are allowed to use.

That *someone* with the task of pointing us to the correct bathroom would probably have a routine job, because usually the determination of one's sex is reasonably evident. The vast majority of the human race has either a penis or a vagina, but not both; or hair or boobs on the chest, but not both. What about the minority, those who have parts from both sexes? Maybe they just have to hold it all in until that *someone* makes a thorough examination of their junk. They could explode while waiting for *someone* to give them the green light. (Occurs to me there could be something more dangerous than suicide bombers.) As an aside, folks who don't believe that some people have both male and female parts should do a Google search. Even as elementary school students attending the little red brick Kuroki School, we had some clues about sexual diversity simply by viewing photos of hermaphrodites in Encyclopedia Britannica. Medicine and science have shown that sexuality is governed even more by brain functions and hormonal activity than by external body parts. We know that not all bodies fit neatly into male and female categories. Could it be that our brains and hormones are similarly diverse?

But I digress. Those misguided politicians, wanting to legislate where people can poop and pee, have unwittingly turned half their constituents into criminals. I speak here of senior citizens. For older folks, finding an available washroom becomes a matter of some urgency. If the washroom deemed appropriate for my sex is occupied, and I have an uncontrollable urge to drain my bladder, I have been known to discreetly and furtively enter the forbidden sanctuary of the "ladies' room". My wife is complicit in this criminal activity. She stands by the door to warn any entering females of my unlawful occupation of "their" premises. We are in this together. I have done the same for her. We are both guilty and deserve whatever punishment the courts impose.

When I enter a public washroom, I am constantly looking over my shoulder fearing that the Poop Policeman or the Defecation Detection Detective is watching my every move. Seniors have been known to be in such a rush that they unwittingly enter the wrong bathroom. I know I have. On one occasion, at an RV Park, I unwittingly entered the wrong bathroom, couldn't find a urinal, did my job in a toilet cubicle and commenced shaving. Within a few seconds, a person of the opposite sex came out of the shower room chastising me for using the ladies' room. I hurriedly and embarrassingly apologized and scurried out. Fortunate for me that I was not imprisoned for my misdemeanour. One wonders if our nation's jail cells will be filled with seniors found guilty of bathroom crimes against humanity. But that would solve the problem. Any photos I have seen of jail cells always show a toilet right within the cell. No worries about whether one is male, female, transgender or anywhere else along the sexual diversity continuum. Aside from our own homes, prison might be the only place where we can poop in peace. Only one problem left: if I am a male or transgender guilty of using the women's washroom, will I be locked up in the men's prison or the women's prison? Or will they be doing strip searches to determine my true sex?

I know, you're asking yourself what all this has to do with religion. But I'm asking myself, "Where are the religious leaders who ought to be speaking out loudly, vociferously and courageously supporting the rights of human beings in a natural function so basic as being able to use the bathroom without being harassed?" What would Jesus say about the mistreatment of our fellow humans, alive among us, dying a thousand deaths daily because they are misunderstood, maligned, tortured and even killed because of their sexual orientation?

What would Jesus do? What will I do? What would I do if my son or daughter, niece or nephew, grandson or granddaughter "came out" with non-traditional sexuality? Would I accept and love them? Or would I vote for the politicians who revile them? Jesus' admonition to love and the statement of the *Golden Rule* contain no limitations regarding race, skin colour, sexual orientation, mental or physical disability, or any other perceived difference. Everyone is someone's son or daughter.

Rather than focusing on preventing specific individuals from using certain bathrooms could our society focus on ways to make all bathrooms gender neutral? Here is what Jack Antonoff said about this matter: "*Anyone who is awake and aware knows that these quote-unquote bathroom bills or any legislation discriminating against LGBTQ citizens is horrible".*

Chapter 18
Celibacy, a Catholic Conundrum

"If, hypothetically, Western Catholicism were to review the issue of celibacy, I think it would do so for cultural reasons, not so much as a universal option." - Pope Francis

There's a crack in the doorway. At least the Pope is willing to talk about celibacy. But from my own experience, I believe change will be a long time coming. The Catholic Church hierarchy as well as laity are very slow to change. For example, when the Church finally adopted the use of the vernacular in the celebration of the Mass in 1965, other new practices were introduced. One of these was that the use of the Communion Rail was abandoned. Prior to 1965, recipients of the Eucharist would kneel in a line at the "Communion Rail" in front of the altar.

The priest would walk along placing the Host on the tongue of each person. The new practise, and one which is still in vogue, was that the priest would stand in front of the altar while the laity would stand in line, coming forward one at a time to receive the Host in the palm of their hand. The communion recipient would then place the Host in their own mouth and reverently consume it. Easier said than done! There have been, and always will be traditionalists who believe every change is a sacrilege. I recall one older woman who refused to follow the new practice, engaging in a running verbal battle with the parish priest about what a sin it was for people not to kneel and to have the audacity to touch the Communion with their hand. She continued to kneel at the Communion Rail and would not accept the Communion Host in her hand. Rather than refuse to give her Communion, the priest acceded to her intransigence.

If small changes are difficult to implement, what chance is there for the marriage of priests? There are likely no theological reasons for prohibiting their marriage. There was no rule of celibacy in the early days of the church. It was not until the Second Lateran Council held in 1139 that a rule was approved forbidding priests to marry. In fact, although it is not widely known, there currently are many married Roman Catholic priests, and there are certainly married clergy in many Christian and non-Christian faiths. There have even been legally married Popes: Pope Hormisdas (514-523), Pope Adrian II (867-872), Pope John XVII (1003) and Pope Clement IV (1265-1268).

My own feeling is that Catholic priests ought not to be held to a vow of celibacy. Perhaps I have been slightly biased in this regard. One of my cousins, who entered the priesthood, and whom I regarded as an excellent preacher, teacher and pastor, left the priesthood to get married. He was not alone. In August 2018 Keysel Besa wrote an article in *"the gateway"*, entitled: *Mandatory celibacy is crippling the Catholic Church.* In the article, Keysel notes that in America alone, approximately 25,000 priests have left their jobs to marry. What makes this fact so devastating and even hypocritical is the little-known fact that there are several married Roman Catholic priests in the USA. According to an article from March 18, 2017 in the California Catholic Daily there are as many as 120 married priests in America, most of them having converted from the Episcopalian faith as a result of a 1980 offer by Pope John Paul II for married Episcopal priests to continue their ministry after converting to Catholicism. The article features Father Paul Sullins, a former Episcopal priest who was ordained in the Catholic Church in 2002. A married man with three grown children, Father Sullins is the pastor of St. Mark the Evangelist Catholic Church in Hyattsville, Maryland. According to Sullins, couples feel more comfortable coming to him knowing that he can relate more closely to their issues. In fact, he and his wife sometimes co-counsel couples with marital problems.

SOOOOOooooo, in North America, Catholics who become priests cannot marry. Yet Episcopalians who are married Episcopal priests can become Catholic priests. Moreover, certain rites of Roman Catholicism in Europe permit the marriage of priests. In fact, in the little town of Norquay, Saskatchewan, where my parents lived for many years, there was an immigrant Catholic priest who came from Europe with a wife and child. The enthusiasm with which he and his little family were welcomed into the community makes one wonder at the wisdom of the celibacy rule.

At one time or another, every human being and every human institution makes faulty decisions which result in catastrophic consequences, even if their intentions might be honourable. Is this the case with the policy of mandatory celibacy for *most* Catholic clergy? It is an extremely questionable practice, contributing to an aura of exclusivity, pride and superiority in direct contradiction with Jesus' teachings. Moreover, it creates unwarranted daily pressure on Catholic priests to be something that most cannot be. Most will admit to sexual desire, and those who are honest will confess to succumbing to sexual urges. That is not to say that celibacy is wrong. For a small minority of individuals of unusually diminished libido, it may be more suitable than marriage or sexual dalliance. But is it dangerous to create an exclusive old boys club purporting to live up to the improbable lofty ideals of complete celibacy?

It is a huge leap to assume that allowing priests to marry or accepting that God created human beings with a wide spectrum of sexual orientations would eliminate every sexual dalliance ascribed to religious leaders. However, the repression of all sexual urges in Catholic clergy could be a contributing factor in many high-profile sexual scandals. Yet despite all evidence, the Catholic Church's hierarchy refuses to acknowledge the appropriateness of sexual intimacy for its clergy. According to Maslow's hierarchy of needs, deficiencies in basic human needs of food and water, warmth, shelter and sexual intimacy create anxiety and neurotic behaviours. The following news items provide some evidence of neurotic, deviant and even criminal behaviour:

The *National Catholic Reporter* article from April 2010 entitled: Secret sex in the celibate system.

A January 2017 edition of a CBC program, *The Current* notes that many Vatican observers, such as Thomas Reese, a Jesuit priest and *National Catholic Reporter* columnist very bluntly states, "The idea that gays cannot be good priests is stupid, demeaning, unjust, and contrary to the facts," wrote Reese. "I know many very good priests who are gay, and I suspect even more good priests I know are gay."

An August 2018 report in *The Inquirer*, a Philadelphia Newspaper: Top Roman Catholic leaders in Pennsylvania covered up decades of child sex abuse involving more than 1,000 victims and hundreds of priests, according to a long-awaited grand jury report.

A *CBS News* headline from February 2019: Pope says priests' abuse of nuns went as far as "sexual slavery"

A *New York Times* headline from February 2019: Nun's Rape Case Against Bishop Shakes a Catholic Bastion in India

This is just a small sample. The reader has heard of, or regrettably, maybe even experienced, similar cases in their own community. Sex is a natural human impulse – it cannot be totally suppressed without dire consequences - which both the Church and society in general have been unable to tackle in a sensible manner. That is not to say that permitting priests to marry would eliminate all problems relating to sex. Sexuality, sexual urges and sexual impropriety are a human condition as evidenced by problems of divorce, separation, extra-marital affairs and scandals in all religions as well as among politicians and the general public. Does mandatory celibacy create an extra layer of potential sexual tension and unacceptable behaviours in those who are priests?

Subsequent to the August 2018 revelations of the Philadelphia sex abuse and cover-up scandal involving up to a thousand child victims and hundreds of priest perpetrators, on August 21, 2018, Father Richard Rohr attached a link to his daily meditation where he directly addressed the horrible issue. Thank you to Father Rohr for permitting me to quote his entire statement verbatim:

Fr. Richard's statement on the new revelations of priestly abuse and cover-up:

"This moral catastrophe first of all demands public and sincere lamentation from every segment of the Body of Christ, and only then can the deep healing begin. It also demands public ownership, repentance and reform of our very immature teaching in regard to sexuality in general, male power issues in particular, and our "enforced" understanding of celibacy, which will predictably produce this kind of result.

Our own Catholic theology says that celibacy is a "charism" which means a free and empowered gift. In my experience, only someone who has an alive and warm inner experience of God is capable of celibacy at all.

It is a contradiction in terms for the Catholic Church to think it can mandate a free gift, which of course, has no precedent in Jesus. It is clearly not necessary for ministry, and is often a liability, creating an aura of spiritual superiority when the exact opposite is often the case.

I personally believe the actual charism of male celibacy that produces both happy and healthy men by the second half of life, is quite rare.

Until the Catholic Church disconnects celibacy from ministry, I think we will continue to have ordained men, who are both unhappy, unhealthy, and a scandal to the Body of Christ. (Lest anyone think incorrectly, I am not saying that celibacy causes pedophilia, but I am saying that the idealized culture of celibacy allowed it to hide there for a long time.) This shadowy material will keep emerging unless we own it and hold it fully accountable. In the meantime, let's all pray and try to live more authentic sexual and spiritual lives ourselves."

A few years prior to the revelation of the shocking and regrettable Philadelphia sexual abuse scandal I posted a blog on this very topic. At that time, I imagined sending a letter to Pope Francis. Father Richard Rohr's bold statement spurred me to action resulting in this September 16, 2018 letter which I sent directly to the Vatican:

September 16, 2018
Gerald Sliva
Winnipeg, MB
R3X 1H5

His Holiness, Pope Francis
Apostolic Palace
00120 Vatican City

Dear Pope Francis,
Peace be with you! I was going to phone you and ask for an audience for me and my coffee buddies, but I understand you are a busy man, so I'll try to make this brief.
The issue of priestly celibacy perplexes us to no end. Celibacy may be an admirable state of life for an occasional priest, or maybe even a lay person. Sex does divert one's attention from prayer and contemplation; yet

the release of sexual tensions also frees one to concentrate on loftier matters, matters not of the flesh, but of the spirit.

There is a growing shortage of Catholic priests, particularly in North America. We know that thousands of Catholic priests have left the priesthood to get married. Many of these married priests were fine pastors, distinguished speakers and respected Church leaders. Many would eagerly return to their priestly duties were they permitted to do so, and many would be eagerly welcomed back by their congregations. We are not biblical scholars and we are certainly not experts on Church law, but we know that there are married priests in certain rites or branches of the Catholic Church. We also know that in the United States of America certain Episcopalian parishes with married priests have been permitted to become full members of the Catholic faith. Priests have not always been celibate. The twelve apostles were not all celibate. Over the course of history there have been marriages of priests permitted. Celibacy has been a long tradition in the Catholic Church. In the Bible, the Pharisees were known for upholding traditions and concentrating on those traditions and rituals rather than on matters of the spirit. Jesus sometimes had some harsh words for Pharisees. So, is priestly celibacy a necessary tradition or is it a hindrance to the Church?

What would Jesus do?

What will Pope Francis do? The Church has long needed a leader who reflects Jesus' message of love. It is a tough job, but in the brief time you have been the leader we have seen forgiveness rather than judgment, love rather than suspicion and reconciliation rather than division.

Thank you, Your Holiness, for listening. May God bless you in your good work.

Peace be with you.

Yours truly,
Gerald M. Sliva

As yet, I have not received a reply. I do not expect one. It matters not. Simply knowing that many clergy and lay persons in the church have similar opinions leaves me with hope for some change in the future.

However, celibacy in the priesthood is just the tip of the conundrum iceberg. There appears to be a hodgepodge of rules depending upon the religion or sex of the prospective Roman Catholic priest. I wonder if a currently married Catholic priest could become Pope. Then, since married *male* Episcopalian priests are welcomed as Catholic priests, perhaps female Episcopal priests should be afforded the same option. Then, if female priests, what about a female Pope? Did Jesus ever say, "Keep the women out!"? Are all these rules theologically based or are they simply designed to keep females out of the Vatican power structure? Sooner or later I believe these issues will be addressed in a manner which reflects the application and acceptance of the *Golden Rule*. (Not likely in my lifetime.)

Part 5 – Prayer

"Prayer is about knowing God – not manipulating Him." – Tom Blackaby

Gerald M. Sliva

Chapter 19
Thy Kingdom Come

"Prayer is not asking. It is a longing of the soul. It is a daily admission of one's weakness. It is better in prayer to have a heart without words than words without a heart." - Mahatma Gandhi

Jesus said it a little differently when the apostles asked Jesus to teach them to pray, but the message is the same: "In your prayers do not babble as the pagans do, for they think that by using many words they will make themselves heard. Do not be like them; your Father knows what you need before you ask him." - Matthew 6:8

Jesus then went on to teach us how to pray. He gave us the words, but is our heart there too? I've been thinking about, analyzing and examining the most common prayer of Christians, the prayer Jesus gave us, *The Lord's Prayer*.

I know the prayer well. You do too. Maybe I mouth the words (babble on?) without truly considering their importance. Maybe I ought to reflect on the meaning of those words, to put my heart into the prayer.

"*Our Father who art in heaven*", so far, I am on solid ground. If I regard God as the Father of all humans, and I accept all people of all races, colours, ethnic origins and cultures as my brothers and sisters, He is *OUR* Father. I recognize God as our Father, Creator, the Supreme Being and Loving Force who resides in a very special place.

But then, am I really sure I mean the next line, "*Hallowed be Thy Name.*"? Do I really keep God's name holy? Or even intend to do so? On the streets, in movies, in restaurants and coffee shops I commonly hear cursing and swearing, using God's Holy Name with everything but reverence and holiness. Confession time: I have been guilty.

As children, we heard crude language, and we often aped what we heard. We didn't always know how unsophisticated, crude and disrespectful foul language was. And even if we knew, we thought it was cool to test the limits of our new-found vocabulary. I am far from being a saint, and in relapse times, I have been known to use foul language, but I very purposely refrain from using God's Name in vain. It was my fortune to have had a good example in this regard. Never once in my life did I hear my own father disrespect the name of God.

Just a few more lines into our prayer: "*Thy kingdom come. Thy will be done on earth as it is in Heaven.*" Here again, I can very easily become hypocritical. Do I ***really*** want God's will to be done on earth? God has given humans free will, free choice to do good or evil. Do I really want God's kingdom on earth and am I working toward it? If I am honest, in the last election, did I vote for the party and the person who is most likely to do God's will? What would the government of God look like? Doubtful it would even remotely resemble the majority of current administrations. God's kingdom is one of loving, accepting, forgiving and helping all who are in need: prostitutes, drug addicts, thieves, beggars, immigrants, minorities, the poor, the lame, and the forgotten. "Whatsoever you do to these, the least of my brothers and sisters, you do unto me." My own observation, sadly even some of my own practice, has been that we really don't want God's will to be done on earth. We want our own will to be done - that's our goal and object of our striving. And if our will isn't done, we pout, throw a tantrum or complain that God isn't answering OUR prayers. Maybe John Ruskin said it best: "If you do not wish for His kingdom, don't pray for it. But if you do, you must do more than pray for it, you must work for it."

"*Give us this day our daily bread,*" Finally, an easy line. I am asking and trusting God to grant me the things I really need each day.

"*And forgive us our trespasses, as we forgive those who trespass against us.*" Whoa! Can I really mean that? I am asking God to treat me the way I treat others when they make a mistake, when they sin against me. Am I being a hypocrite when I pray those words? If I can't forgive my wife, my friend, my associate, or if I hold a grudge, am I asking God to hold a grudge against me when I make a mistake? That's what the words appear to say.

Forgiveness can be so difficult when I feel unappreciated and ignored. These are tiny hurts. But most of us have never been truly tested. Would I ever be able to forgive someone who murdered a loved one: a spouse, a brother, sister, father or mother, a grandchild? I pray that would never happen,

but I wonder how eager I would be to say, "Father, forgive them, for they know not what they do."?
"And lead us not into temptation, but deliver us from evil. Amen." Wow! I did it! I prayed the prayer Jesus taught me. And it took a whole twenty-five or thirty seconds of my life. The sacrifices I'll make for my Creator!

Gerald M. Sliva

Chapter 20
Prayers of Charity

"I tell you solemnly, in so far as you did this to one of the least of these brothers of mine, you did to me" - Matthew 25:40

I am on this earth for a few short years. I really own nothing. What I call *my* possessions are only lent to me for as long as I am alive and cling to them, or until I leave this earth. It is true that I can't take them with me. Then why am I here? What is my purpose in life? Is it to accumulate baubles which give transitory pleasure? Or is it to have the imagination, vision and spirit of giving, of charity, and of helping others? Does it really matter why I give or what I give? Is it more important to give my treasures of time, or my prayers, or my treasures of worldly goods? Or might I give all three of the above? Is it more important to give because of Jesus' urging, out of feelings of guilt, out of love for fellow creatures, or even for the hope or promise of some future reward, perchance Heaven? The great humanitarian, physician and philosopher, Albert Schweitzer, modelled his life after the example and teachings of Jesus even though he did not regard Jesus as the Saviour, the Christ or as God. His idea was that true charity and altruism involved giving for the "love and reverence for life" and not for any good feeling or hope of reward. He promoted love and respect for all life (human, animal, as well as insect and plant) as his primary motivation for giving his life's work to help the poor and destitute in the jungles of Africa.

There are needs in Africa as well as right where we live, in our hometowns. My coffee buddies and I have solved many problems in the world, but the constant reality of poverty, panhandlers and beggars in a wealthy country leaves us bewildered. The global societal issues which contribute to destitution, disease, disability, bankruptcy, starvation, malnutrition and the resulting desperation are all to blame for putting beggars on our streets. Mental and physical illness, drug abuse, war, greed, alcoholism, gambling, racism and government inaction are just a few of the problems which lead desperate people to resort to the desperate measures of living on the streets as vagabonds, tramps, mendicants and dumpster divers. The causes of these concerns are the subjects of much controversy and debate which I do not intend to address here. What I wish to address is this fact: the poor are with us. Doing *nothing* is not an option. What I, as an individual and we as a society do about it defines our humanity.

Mother Teresa's favourite response, when asked why she worked with the destitute on the streets of Calcutta, was to quote Matthew 25:40, "I tell you solemnly, in so far as you did this to one of the least of these brothers of mine, you did to me."

My own response has sometimes been less than charitable. Sometimes, when encountered, I have avoided eye contact with a panhandler – that solves the problem, Eh? I can blame the individual for their condition. They made bad choices and are now suffering their deserved consequences. The decision has been made. Ignore him/her and simply bemoan the conditions which have led an individual to wander the streets begging for their next meal. I have other options, you know. There are differences of opinion about what course of action is best for the individual and for society. Whole television and radio talk shows have discussed it; newspaper editorials abound. One side says by giving the beggar a handout we are merely perpetuating a problem and encouraging more of the behaviour – begging. The other side says that we should not judge. Someone needs help – give it.

In 1995 my son, Greg and I did some bonding by taking a trip together to Las Vegas. We spent three days seeing the sights, relaxing and doing a minor amount of gambling. One morning, as we walked to a fast food restaurant for a breakfast snack, we happened upon a youngish looking fellow, maybe about thirty-five years old, asking for a handout. Maybe I was thinking "Matthew 25:40", maybe I just wanted to be a bit charitable, or maybe I just wanted to put him off; but I thought to myself, "We are in Las Vegas, the gaming capital of North America. If I give the fellow a cash donation, he'll just go to the nearest casino, risk it on a spin of the slots or a throw of the dice and he'll be no better off than if I had done nothing." So, priding myself on being a frugal, conservative, yet magnanimous humanitarian I suggested to him that we were going for breakfast, and if he was hungry, I would be pleased to buy him a breakfast equivalent to what we were having. He agreed, ordered his breakfast, sat a few tables away from us and then he had second thoughts. In a loud voice he commenced berating me, saying that I did a stupid thing by not giving him cash with which he could have gone to the grocery store, using the money to buy some bacon and eggs, with which he could have fed his whole family.

Initially, I was extremely put off by his attitude. I felt I had helped the fellow, and now he was telling me off. Is that any way to treat your benefactor? I wanted to tell him how I felt, and discussed doing so with my son who wisely advised me to simply let the fellow vent as I had nothing to gain by debating with him or scolding him for his bad attitude. I could have figuratively shot my mouth off, venting back at him. But in the USA, people have been known to carry guns, so he could have literally shot my mouth off. I just sat quietly, grumbling to Greg about the ingrate, avoiding both figurative and literal gunplay.

Over the years, I have related this incident to many people, invariably portraying myself as the beneficent, charitable, caring humanitarian and the beggar as the spoiled brat. I was the good guy; he was the villain. Maybe I've mellowed, softened my stance a bit. What if the fellow was right? What if I deprived a family of an opportunity to share a meal? Maybe I'm not the hero in this story. My current opinion is that if I decide to give a beggar a handout, it is a gift without conditions. I cannot judge his true need. Maybe he needs a cigarette or a drink of alcohol to help him survive another day on the streets. Maybe he needs a meal for himself, a few litres of milk for his hungry child – that is not for me to judge. My only decision is to give or to withhold.

A few years ago, I decided to take giving to a more personal level. One day I reached the decision to do this when I saw a homeless person begging for loose change. Deciding that the beggar needed the money more than I did, I gave him a five-dollar bill. Since that time, I try to keep a small supply of five-dollar bills in my vehicle as well as in my wallet for the express purpose of giving to beggars. Every time I give out five dollars, this is my thought: "He/she needs it more than I do." Is it the *right* thing to do? Am I contributing to delinquency? I am conflicted about my own practice. Maybe there's a better way. One of my friends keeps a supply of granola bars in his vehicle. When he sees a panhandler, he offers a bar. Perhaps that's a better route. To be clear about this, I'm no hero in this endeavour. Living in a more affluent, middle class neighbourhood, I encounter panhandlers only two or three times a month unless I venture into the downtown or core areas of our city. How long would I be charitable if I met four, five or more beggars each day? I wonder!

Rethinking my whole approach, I considered whether my five dollars is having any appreciable longer-term benefit for the recipient. Probably not! To try to be more proactive, with some hope of providing longer term assistance, I try to attach a small piece of paper with the address and telephone number of the Siloam Mission soup kitchen to each five-dollar bill. Siloam is a fine organization, helping many homeless citizens with food, clothing, shelter, warmth and counselling each day. I provide direct financial support to Siloam knowing that their organization does much better work and provides more lasting benefit than a small handout ever will.

There are more ways to help than just giving cash. In *Albert Schweitzer, A study of his philosophy of life* by

Gabriel Langfeldt and translated from Norwegian by Maurice Michael, he outlines Schweitzer saying as much: "*Open your eyes says the true ethic, and see if you cannot find a person or some philanthropic work that needs some of your time, kindliness, sympathy and effort. Perhaps there is an ill or a bitter or a lonely or helpless person to whom you can be something. An old person, perhaps, or a child.*" Charitable organizations need volunteers. Many of my friends and acquaintances work regular shifts at Siloam Mission and other charities, help to sponsor refugees, support third world orphanages, raise money for charities and do other personal good deeds.

My personal belief is that we are all called to perform some form of charity. We can give all kinds of reasons or excuses for not helping those in need: it creates dependency; the CEO's of large charities receive outrageous salaries; a large percentage of funds raised are spent on administration and fundraising rather than on helping the needy. I can conjure up many more excuses for not giving, but perhaps it is my responsibility to find one of the many charities which do admirable work and contribute at least a portion of my treasures of time and money. Or if I can't find a suitable charity, maybe I should start one on my own. The need is there.

One of my friends – I'll call him Adam (not his real name) - has embodied Schweitzer's philosophy and has taken charity to a very personal level. He noted that one of his neighbours, aged 90, appeared to be having serious health problems. Alone, his home unsanitary and apparently with no support systems, he needed help. Adam and his wife took charge. They cleaned his house, took him to medical appointments and had him admitted to hospital where he was on the verge of expiring. On a few occasions,

Adam told me that the old fellow was near death. Miracles happen. Adam's friendship and care together with some medication and sustenance from the hospital medical staff soon produced positive results. Adam continues to periodically visit the old fellow in the nursing home where he recently celebrated his ninety-first birthday.

Most human beings, at one time or another need the help of others. In a caring society, the government has a role to play, but leaving it all to government is pure socialism. Leaving it all to the other guy is pure selfishness. Charity is an option. Do you have a story of neighbourly charity, of the *Golden Rule* in action? Do you wish to share it? Please email it to **myconundra@gmail.com**

Where there is natural disaster, economic hardship, physical or mental disability: *"I tell you solemnly, in so far as you did this to one of the least of these brothers of mine, you did to me"* - Matthew 25:40

Chapter 21
Talking With Jesus

I had a little talk with Jesus. He's white, upper-middle class, you know. He speaks English, drives a mid-size Chevy on the right-hand side of the road, and has a conservative stock portfolio.

Jesus Christ was born on Christmas Day,
He grew up having the unmitigated gall, the nerve, to tell us to love our neighbours.
All of them!
Like the lawyer in the parable I ask, "Who is my neighbour?"
Hoping he won't say, "That Muslim fellow there."
Or maybe he won't tell me, "Black lives matter too."
Maybe he won't tell me he's a Jew, and I gotta love Jews.

Gays, transgenders, First Nations Folks, even illegal aliens?
I gotta love them all?
What about the jerk who let his dog poop on my lawn?
Love?
And the guy who cut me off in heavy traffic?
Love?
And I gotta love my enemies, and pray for them?
Jesus, you gotta be kidding!
Love?
Really?
"Yep," He says.
"Love, the greatest of commandments! Live it!"
Here's the problem, Jesus: I would do it, but I can't trust the other guys to reciprocate. So, I'll arm myself and my home, and build up impenetrable national armaments to ensure that *the other guys (the bad guys)*, who don't love me as they love themselves, don't get the upper hand. I can't trust them and love them, but it's their fault.

Pope Francis has suggested that it is better to be an atheist than a hypocritical Christian. Am I a hypocritical Christian if my love is conditional rather than available to all? I am told to love *everyone*, even the unlovable, and to do good to those who hurt me. A very difficult task! Do I have work to do?

Chapter 22
Talking with God

"If the only prayer you ever say in your entire life is 'thank you', it will be enough," Meister Eckhart

Many years ago, I was asked by a person who was experiencing a difficult time, "How do you pray?" I was somewhat taken aback by the question for two reasons. First, I do not consider myself an authority on prayer and second, that the individual would trust my judgment on so personal a matter. Feeling rather inadequate and unqualified to answer such an important question, I fumbled the ball. I remember mentioning something about praise and thanksgiving, but over the years many times since that night, I have reconsidered the question, and my answer. How could I have done more justice in my response? Having had the opportunity to reflect, cogitate and study the weighty matter of prayer, I feel the need to try again.

Prayer is much more universal than one would imagine at first glance. An April 2014 Reader's Digest article entitled "How We Pray" shows that according to the 2010 General Social Survey, 86 percent of Americans pray, with almost 57% doing so at least once a day. Even one in five non-churchgoers, non-religious, atheists and agnostics confess to engaging in daily prayer. Why prayer? At its core, prayer is communication. Most often it involves an effort to establish or maintain a connection with the Eternal, sometimes to request special favours, but more often to worship, praise or thank God. Among atheists and non-believers, prayer is more likely to be concern and caring for loved ones as well as general thanksgiving for family, friends and a good life, not necessarily an invocation to God.

For many of us, our lives are a quest for something more permanent than our earthly existence. Prayer is part of that search. Deep down we know that there is more to human life than three score and ten years, something greater than our bodies and greater even than our minds. Good prayer ought to humble us, as well as lift us up. In prayer, we are humbled by the knowledge that we are an infinitesimally tiny organism in an unfathomably vast universe. Yet we are exalted by the knowledge that we would not exist if we were not loved.

Prayer can take many forms: some involving actions such as performing charitable works, and some involving contemplation, meditation, chanting, dancing, singing or ritual prayer like the Rosary. Depending on the person, their intentions and their circumstances, prayer can involve requesting help, standing in awe of creation, worship, praise, thanksgiving or simply sitting, standing or kneeling in silence, listening for inspiration and guidance. The Catholic Mass is both a prayer and a sacrifice, recalling Jesus' last supper and offering it back to God. When the apostles said to Jesus, "Lord, teach us to pray," Jesus gave us the beautiful Lord's Prayer in which He calls God our Father. It is doubtful, however, that Jesus was inferring the invocation of the Lord's Prayer is the only way to pray. Jesus gave us a terrific example, but God is not so prescriptive that we will act or speak in only one way. We are individuals, each of us with our own unique personality, style, and our own ways of communicating, our own preferences. If God wanted us all to pray in exactly the same way, He would not have made us so diverse. In trying to establish a relationship with God (or anyone, for that matter), maybe words, thoughts and actions other than a repetition of the same words over and over again would be helpful. Prayer is both personal and communal. Devout Muslims pray five times daily. Adherents to the Jewish faith are exhorted to pray three times daily. There is a saying, "He who sings prays twice." There are so many ways to pray, how could I or how should I pray?

I find the daily meditations of Father Richard to be one method of reaching for something beyond the banality of our materialistic society. His perspectives on the values, traditions, spirituality and practises of most religions are a breath of fresh air each day.

So, given our diversity, how could I or how should I pray?

Frankly, I do not know for certain. Uncountable articles and books have been published, and sermons preached on this topic. I can never hope to match them; so, I will dwell on only one manner of prayer, one which I feel brings me closer to God. This method is what I like to call natural or primitive prayer. Sometimes it is planned, but most often it is spontaneous, refreshing and often surprising. It results in a prayer of gratitude or praise for the gift of an awesome experience. Perhaps my most spontaneous *natural prayers* occur in response to my reactions to the wonders of nature. One which I shall never forget occurred on a late autumn fly-in fishing trip with my brother John and my brother-in-law Bruce. We were the only fishermen on beautiful Jean Lake in Northern Saskatchewan. After a successful day of fishing, we beached our boat, enjoyed a leisurely happy hour and prepared our evening meal in the simple accommodations of our shack-tent. The whole day was a prayer. But there was more to come. After eating a delicious meal of beans, fried potatoes and fresh lake trout, the marvel was yet to come. Being early October, the daylight hours were shorter, and the sun set early. After eating, we ventured outdoors in the dark on to the sandy beach to view the marvels of God's creation unimpeded by the electric lights of *civilization*: the lights of uncountable twinkling stars and moon-glow reflections off the mirror-smooth water. Within moments we were treated to an unexpected bonus. Northern lights, the multicoloured aurora borealis danced before us. Far outclassing any man-made fireworks I have ever witnessed, they were completely natural. With iridescent greens, reds, yellows, oranges, blues, purples and every shade of every colour shooting from the highest heavens, down to the lake and tree line, then up again in a celebration of creation and the wonders of nature, the event was surreal, spiritual and breathtaking. For thirty minutes or more we were awestruck. Our prayer was spontaneous and natural. How great Thou art!

I am grateful for having received several of these experiences, some beyond my powers of description. Others which I treasure most are described in the next two chapters entitled *Prayerful Tears* and *Mystical Messages*.

Chapter 23
Prayerful Tears

Our eyes are the windows to our soul; sometimes you gotta wash the windows.

Tears are a natural part of life: a blessing, a spiritual cleansing, and a spontaneous natural prayer of joy or sorrow. I've been thinking about crying - not engaging in the act of crying – at least not at the moment, but rather thinking about what a blessing the act of crying is for human beings. I doubt that anyone ever plans to cry; that is why crying is so terrific. It catches us by surprise and releases our pent-up emotions. Have you had a really good cry recently? If not, you are missing out on life. All the profound moments of our existence are perfect opportunities for the instinctive act of crying: births, weddings, terrific jokes, wonderful surprises, feelings of great loss and sadness, death, grave illness, deep disappointment, true patriotic feelings, love and pride. If you haven't shed a tear or two you've been missing out on some of the most memorable moments of being human. Certainly, we don't want to drag out our crying towel on a daily basis or even weekly or monthly, but occasional crying is mandatory for humanity. That is not to say we yearn for death, illness or great loss, only that when these events enter our lives, as sooner or later they must, the act of crying helps us to reach a state of equilibrium once more. Just as we cannot live in a state of perpetual ecstasy, we cannot live in a state of perpetual grief. Eventually we must return to normalcy or equilibrium. Crying helps us to find that balance in our lives.

When was your last sincere cathartic sobbing? Fortunately for me, I've had more than one. But one sticks out in my mind as an occasion of pure gratitude and joy. It was special, but at the time I was completely unaware. Cecilia and I were at Quail Run RV Park in Arizona on Groundhog Day, February 2, 2014, my seventieth birthday. It was a routine birthday in all respects as far as I knew. Receiving birthday wishes from several friends and neighbours in the RV Park, I felt the day brought little out of the ordinary. In the evening, Cecilia and I went to the recreation centre with some friends for the Saturday night dance.

As we entered the hall looking for a seat, the Needham Twins were on stage preparing to provide us with dance music and entertainment. We like to sit near the back of the hall where the music is not as loud and it is easier to slide in and out of one's seat to go dancing, but to my annoyance someone had plunked a "Reserved" sign on the back table forcing us to take the next table. The band was ready to go and still no one was occupying the "Reserved" table. We settled in next to that table, visiting with our friends, when suddenly the RV Park manager made an announcement that there were some special guests coming to the dance. Would we please welcome them? To my absolute shock and amazement, through the front door walked my sister and her husband, one brother and his wife, another brother and finally our son. I could not believe my eyes. To hugs, kisses and tears of welcome they entered the hall. Unbelievably, the "Reserved" sign was for me and all my relatives. A few minutes later, when I was just regaining my composure, an old school chum and his wife entered to join the celebration. My friends and relatives had travelled from all parts of Canada all the way to Arizona to help me celebrate my seventieth birthday. They brought tequila, rum, rye whisky, beer, munchies and a huge birthday cake which we shared with the hundred or so people in the hall. My relatives had rented a large four-bedroom house near the RV Park, were set to party for the weekend and party we did. After the dance we all crowded into our very small park model trailer where there was another huge surprise and more tears. My other sister and her husband, whose flight from Canada had been delayed, suddenly showed up at our doorstep.

My brother Jim was the instigator, and my wife Cecilia was the co-conspirator of the whole event, keeping the surprise a secret from me for months. Every time that weekend when I considered the thoughtfulness and kindness of my relatives and friends, as well as the huge expense they incurred to help me celebrate my seventieth birthday, tearful prayers of joy and gratitude welled up in me, and remembering it now gives me a repeat performance. Thank you, dear people!

Sadly, there are times when our lives are filled with other tears, tears of sadness, loss, grief and sorrow. The death of my Granny and my Mother were two of these prayerful moments, but there were others, perhaps not as near to me, but still tugging at the floodgates of my heart.

One such occasion, which neither Cecilia nor I will ever forget, was in October 1983. At the time, we lived in Regina, Saskatchewan with our son Greg who was attending the University of Saskatchewan, Regina Campus, taking Honours Chemistry through the co-operative work study program. To his credit, Greg had secured a four-month work-study job at the RCMP Crime Lab in Winnipeg. But when it came time for him to leave home, Cecilia and I had such intense feelings of sadness, emptiness and loss that we literally cried upon his departure and many more times over the next two days. His temporary departure was like a death to us. Who knows why? We had just lived together eating, laughing, vacationing and fighting together for eighteen years. What was the loss? He was just our only living baby leaving us forever!

So, for two days we sulked as we aimlessly roamed around the house quietly mourning our loss, wondering if life would ever be the same. On the second day of our "wake", Cecilia decided to try to distract herself from her grief by raking the front lawn, but as she raked, the tears streamed down her face. At that moment an older neighbour walking his dog chanced upon her sorrow and, noting her sadness, he asked her the cause of her tears. Sobbing, she told him of the temporary departure of our son and our profound sorrow at our loss. His response was simply that he understood her feelings. He and his wife had four grown children and he intimated that with the departure of each youngster they both cried as though their best friend had died.

When Cecilia came back into the house and told me of her encounter with the neighbour, we both had a hearty laugh, more tears, and that was the end of it. After that initial sorrowful departure and eventual return, Greg left us on many occasions for jobs in various places, but never again did we grieve. We celebrated his departures and his returns as beautiful, prayerful parts of our lives.

We have all had a spiritual shedding of precious tears. Sharing tears of joy or sorrow with God or anyone who cares will help to strengthen my relationships and deepen my love. And the sharing of my emotions will strengthen the application of *The Golden Rule* in my everyday life. A Jewish proverb states that what soap is for the body, tears are for the soul. Do prayerful, meditative tears really help to cleanse my soul?

So, I've seen sunshine and I've seen rain; I've experienced great joy and profound grief. They weave an amazing tapestry, our lives of prayerful tears. May your tears be joyful!

Chapter 24
Mystical Messages

The day which we fear as our last is but the birthday of eternity. – Seneca

We, all of us, want to believe in life after death. We want to know for certain that life is something more than just what Shakespeare describes in Act V Scene 5 of *Macbeth*, "Life's but a walking shadow, a poor player that struts and frets his hour upon the stage, and then is heard no more: it is a tale told by an idiot, full of sound and fury, signifying nothing."

We want more. And there is much more. There are supernatural, spiritual or mystical parts of our lives, parts that we do not fully comprehend, parts that we find difficult to discuss. Perhaps it is because they are not of the body, but of the soul. They are ethereal rather than physical. Because they cannot be seen or touched, we tend to be sceptical of their existence, but they are here with us. Not completely trusting the words of the Bible, or Jesus' references to heaven and hell, the Spirit, the supernatural, the unseen world, we search for signs. Certain people, claiming to be mediums, tell us they can receive and interpret messages from the unseen world, from those who have died, or passed to the other side. In fact, Lily Dale, a small hamlet in Western New York is home to a community of fifty-two spiritualists or mediums. Lily Dale attracts about 22,000 visitors each season where one of 52 registered mediums will charge $80 to $100 for a half hour reading. There is a demand. People are interested. Television programs featuring mediums, soothsayers, seers and fortune tellers who purport to be able to communicate with those who have "passed to the other side" are very popular. Are they legitimate, or are they professional scam artists? Although I have received some mysterious signals myself, I am not claiming to have ever heard a direct message from or the voice of any person who is deceased. Also, I am not saying that it is not possible for someone to receive messages from or hear the voice of someone who has passed on. It might be possible. I just don't know.

Further, although I am not one who communicates with the dead, I have a strong belief in God, a Supreme Being, the Giver of all things, the Almighty – I bet you believe in Him too. My belief stems from the observation that this universe, this earth, this body and brain and all of nature are just too marvellous, too amazing and too incomprehensible to have occurred by an accident. So, if God has provided this fantastic life about which we learn and marvel more each day, perhaps billions more amazing discoveries await humankind's discovery, and perchance communication with deceased persons is one of those secrets yet to come. Are you open to it if it comes?

"There are more things in heaven and earth, Horatio, Than are dreamt of in your philosophy."

William Shakespeare, *"Hamlet", Act 1 Scene 5*

I raise these issues because of three interesting experiences I have had. These are not earth-shattering or proof positive of anything, but they are unusual, and they make me think deeply about the quotation from "Hamlet".

My wife, Cecilia and I both have relatives in the Toronto area. Two of my brothers and their families reside there and several of Cecilia's uncles, aunts and cousins are in the area – so we have a lot of relatives there. We visit there occasionally and enjoy packing in a variety of side trips and catching up on family. At one time or another we had visited most of these relatives, but by the time of the first incident, which occurred in 2002, some of the older ones had already been deceased.

In 2002 while we were visiting Cecilia's Uncle Ray, someone suggested that we visit the cemetery where Cecilia's maternal grandfather and grandmother (Ray's parents) were buried. Ray had been there for his parents' funerals and a few times since then, but it was a huge cemetery and when we arrived there, Ray was not exactly sure where the grave sites were located. There were five of us who were making the visit, so Ray pointed us in the appropriate general direction suggesting that we fan out and one of us would likely find the gravestones in short order. For some strange reason though, ignoring his guidance, I was drawn to the North edge of the cemetery. Making a beeline for one spot, I stopped and looked down. At my feet was a brass grave marker inscribed with the names of Michael and Josephine Slobodian.

I was somewhat amazed to find myself there. How and why did I single out that one grave marker out of the many thousands in that cemetery? Michael was a cousin of my mother and I had visited at their home a few times many years prior. I did not even know that they were buried in that cemetery. I felt that they had called me directly to that spot, they wanted a visit, and that is why I had ignored Ray's direction about where to search for his parents' graves. In any event, I had a little visit, said a little prayer, took a photo and returned to where the others had already found Cecilia's grandparent's grave.

I described my experience to those present on that day, and several days later to my siblings, to Mike and Josie's son and to many others who may not have cared. Maybe it was simply a coincidence, but for me it was a spiritual experience.

The second incident or coincidence occurred in Clearwater, British Columbia. My Uncle Mike Mazer, an aging bachelor uncle, had asked my cousin and me to be executors for his last will and testament. Uncle Mike had died on July 27, 2006 so my cousin and I hurriedly travelled together from Winnipeg, Manitoba to Clearwater, B.C. to commence settling Uncle Mike's estate and to hold a small memorial service for him. For several hectic days we cleaned his small mobile home residence, selling some items, giving away others and making many trips to the landfill with items not wanted.

We had made arrangements with the local parish priest to hold a small community memorial service in conjunction with the regular Saturday evening Mass at the Catholic Church of St. James in Clearwater on Saturday, August 5, 2006 in the late afternoon. Uncle Mike had been a faithful attendee at the parish, and the ladies of the parish graciously volunteered to provide a lunch after the memorial service.

My cousin and I were the only relatives of Uncle Mike at the remote community of Clearwater. Having previously arranged for his remains to be cremated, a few hours before the memorial service, we travelled to the local funeral home to pick up the urn containing Uncle Mike's ashes. Then we had some time on our hands. Not being in a situation like this before and not knowing what to do, we simply returned to our motel room to sit and wait until the service would begin. There the two of us sat on the motel room bed, quietly meditating, with Uncle Mike's urn on the small side table beside us. After some time of reverent silence, I suggested we turn the radio on to search for some quiet music. My cousin immediately turned on the radio and we heard the haunting strains of the Sons of the Pioneers singing *Cool Clear Water*. Here we were in Clearwater, B.C. and the song being played was Clear Water. That was a bit of a coincidence, but something much more unusual struck me, and to describe why, I must relate an incident from the early 1950's.

Uncle Mike had been in partnership with my Dad; together they owned Kuroki Hotel. However, wanting more adventure, Uncle Mike sold his share in the hotel to my Dad, striking out on his own by securing a job in a gold mine in Uranium City, a small fly-in community on Lake Athabasca in Northern Saskatchewan. Before he left, he gave me and my brother a small old black suitcase containing a wind-up gramophone together with a couple old 78 rpm records. One I will never forget was a song by the Sons of the Pioneers, *Cool Clear Water*. As seven and eight-year-old children, my brother Don and I cranked up that old gramophone and played the scratched up 78 rpm record over and over until we finally wore out the gramophone spring and the old 78 rpm record. For me, hearing that song again, that song given to me by Uncle Mike with Uncle Mike's ashes sitting between my cousin and me was pure reverence. It was a message from Uncle

Mike that he had come to his resting place of green meadows and Cool Clear Water.

So, for a second time I felt blessed and tearfully related my experience to those present at the memorial service and then again by email to all my cousins who were co-heirs to Uncle Mike's estate and to many others later. It was truly a mystical experience for me.

My third and most recent experience of this nature was the most vivid. It involved Evelyn, who is my sister-in-law, and her husband Don, who is my brother, from Concord, Ontario. Stricken with leukemia, Evelyn was quite weak after having undergone chemotherapy; by October 2011 she had lost all her hair and was convalescing at home while awaiting the results of her chemotherapy to determine if it had produced the desired result. Since it was a very difficult time for Evelyn and my brother Don, we tried to provide what long distance moral support we were able by telephone, greeting cards and Skype. On one occasion while Evelyn was home and being visited by my brother Jim and his wife Shannon, we managed to connect via Skype and had a pleasant, uplifting visit even though Evelyn was in seriously deteriorating health. During that visit I took a Skype photo of Don, Evelyn, Jim and Shannon.

For a few weeks longer, Evelyn remained at home only to receive the news that the chemotherapy had not eradicated her leukemia forcing her to return to the hospital with the choices of either undergoing another round of excruciatingly agonizing chemo or facing the end of her life. The proposed new round of powerful chemo was partially experimental desperation, only being used successfully on a few occasions in the United States. Evelyn was willing to undergo this risky chemotherapy primarily because the objective was to eradicate her body of the leukemia, then to implant bone marrow from her brother, Reg who was a perfect match for her. Unfortunately, in Evelyn's weakened physical condition, the powerful chemotherapy simply wracked her body with painful sores, swelling and open wounds. The news from my brother Don was rather bleak. We knew that Evelyn did not have long in this world.

On the morning of November 21, 2011 at 4:03 a.m. I awoke from a deep sleep. Hearing the unique ringing of the special Skype ringtone I had downloaded from the internet, I bolted upright in bed so suddenly that I awakened Cecilia who asked me what was happening. I told her someone was calling us on Skype, but the moment I said it, I remembered that our computer had been turned off for the night, making it impossible for Skype to be activated. Immediately, I was convinced that Evelyn had called via "heaven sent Skype" to let us know that she was now at peace and that she had made it safely to the other side. Waiting for what I expected to be the inevitable contact from my brother Don, the rest of that night I tossed and turned, absolutely certain of Evelyn's passing. Knowing in my heart what had happened, the next morning I checked my email and saw a message from Don that Evelyn had passed away earlier that morning. When I next had telephone contact with him, I described what had happened to me, shortly thereafter sharing the same information with all my siblings and close cousins via email. As with the two prior experiences, I felt a profound sense of gratitude at being granted the privilege of receiving what I regard as mystical messages.

The following is an unedited copy of the email which I sent to my relatives on that day. I thank my sister Barbara for retrieving this email for me from her archived in-basket as I had long ago trashed my original.

Sent: Monday, November 21, 2011 1:19:24 PM
Subject: Spiritual experience
Hello my dear relatives:
I had a very interesting experience last night. I feel compelled to share it with you. With the passing of our dear Sister-in-Law, Evelyn, we will all consider our own mortality and go through mourning. Sometimes we go through rituals and "hope" there is an afterlife, but sometimes we find it hard to truly "believe" with all our beings that there is an afterlife.
So, this is what happened: This morning at 4:03 A.M. Toronto time I bolted upright in bed with such intensity that I woke Cecilia. She asked me what was wrong, and I told her I heard the Skype phone ringing. (Both our computers were off.) At that moment, I felt that Evelyn was making a Skype call to give us a message that she was entering a new life.
I didn't sleep much the rest of the night and I was apprehensive about checking the email this morning, but when I did, I was quite certain what news I would find. You may believe what you wish, but I believe there are many things we do not understand in life or in death, so I wanted to share my spiritual experience with you.
May God's Peace be with you and yours.
Love,
Gerald

    At Evelyn's funeral service on November 24, 2011 in the North part of Toronto, I tearfully recounted my receiving the Skype call from Evelyn on the early morning of her journey into the afterlife.

Peace be to the three relatives who favoured me with messages from beyond. Each of you is a treasure to my memory.

(On a lighter note, on one occasion I described these incidents to my three brothers. My youngest brother, John, asked if I really believed that I received a Skype call from Evelyn when she was passing from this life. I told him, "Yes!"

His response to me: "If you get a Skype call from me, hang up!")

I have had other experiences which even more vividly illustrate my belief in the hereafter, God and the spirit world. I know that many of you have too. Those experiences are a gift. I would love to hear your stories if you are inclined to share them. To contact me please email me at myconundra@gmail.com.

Part 6 – After Life

"When you realize that other dimensions exist, you'll never think of life, death, yourself, or the universe in the same way again." – The Afterlife of Billy Fingers, a true story by Annie Kagan

Chapter 25
Eternal Cosmic Suits

"We are not human beings on a spiritual journey. We are spiritual beings on a human journey." — Steven Covey

Today I read a touching true story about a father taking his disabled, dying son on a fishing excursion. The father, observing his son's painful struggle with the fishing rod, burst into tears.

"Dad," the son said, "Why are you crying? There's nothing wrong with me. It's just my Earth suit that's having trouble. There's nothing wrong with me."

Reading those lines caused me some serious reflection. Very rarely are we willing to reveal our true selves, our cosmic suits, the ones that hold our spirit. It's not *cool* to do so. But, if we are at peace with ourselves, our fellow humans and with our Creator, is there really nothing wrong with us? No matter the condition of our Earth suits, are we okay?

In the following little poem, who is speaking? If I believe in God, a Creator, could I imagine the Creator speaking? Could it be a disabled panhandler, or a prostitute, a friend, a neighbour or a spouse who is speaking? Maybe I am speaking?

My Earth Suit

Who am I?
I am not who people see.
They only see my Earth suit
whether it be white, black, brown or yellow.
They only see my outward self: my scars, my limp, my
scruffy beard, my toothless grin, my tears, my ugliness.
They only see, judge and shun my crutch, my fault, my
imperfection.
They don't see me.
They only see my Earth suit, my outward self: my flawless
skin, my flowing hair
my ruby lips, my radiant smile, my pearly teeth
my round, full breasts
my shapely legs, my beauty.
They only see my Earth suit, and gawk and leer and lust
for me.
They don't see me.
They don't know me.
I am not who people see.
Who am I?

We imperfect humans often judge others, and even ourselves, by outward appearances. Yet we know there is so much more to humanity than our Earth suits. Perhaps each of us has another suit, an eternal Cosmic suit, one of beauty, light and joy, which we will someday unabashedly display to the world.

Can I use true discernment to see beyond externals, to see the reality of each person I encounter? Can I do the same to see the beauty in all Creation? Can I see beyond my own and my neighbours' Earth suit?

Gerald M. Sliva

Chapter 26
Our Bodies are Caterpillars; Our Souls, Butterflies

We can scarce believe the miracle of life. Perhaps that is why we find it so difficult to believe in the miracle of afterlife.

As we age, we get a changing perspective of life and death. Assuming we have good health, we might like to live a life span of one hundred years. We aren't satisfied with the three score and ten mentioned in the Bible. So, one hundred years might not be unreasonable given the improvements to health care and technological assists to our physical and mental well-being. If, like me, you are over fifty years of age, the countdown to one hundred has begun. Life might be closer to ending and death might be closer to beginning. We would be lying if we didn't admit that we ask questions more often about what happens after we kick the proverbial bucket. What happens *after life*? Does our existence cease? If we continue to exist, what form do we take? Is there a heaven? Is there a hell? What are they like? Will we meet God face to face? Will we understand, at least a little bit, the mysteries of the universe? Will we truly have no more troubles and no more tears? Will it be everlasting? Everlasting is a long time. Will we get tired and bored with "forever"?

Perhaps *afterlife* is a misnomer. Life does not end. It is merely transformed. *"The fact that life and death are not two is extremely difficult to grasp, not because it is so complex, but because it is so simple."* - Ken Wilber, *The Spectrum of Consciousness*. Jesus told us the same, in different words, "Unless a grain of wheat falls to the ground and dies, it shall remain but a single grain" – that grain of wheat really doesn't die. It changes. It multiplies or becomes enhanced and reproduces itself in a miraculous fashion. Nature demonstrates that in countless other marvellous ways. Take the lowly caterpillar, for instance, transforming itself into the wondrous butterfly. Same creature – different form. Scientists have proven that the caterpillar and the butterfly even have the same DNA and that the butterfly remembers being a caterpillar. Imagine the memories of the resurrected butterfly, recalling its existence as a lowly caterpillar, crawling, grovelling, consuming rotting leaves and fruit and vegetables, or even decaying human and animal flesh. One day it wraps itself in a cocoon, only to awaken, miraculously finding that it can fly, no longer tethered to the earth. It is no longer eating vegetation, leftovers, carrion and garbage. The caterpillar can scarce believe that it is free to soar where it wills, free to visit flower after glorious flower, feasting on the nectar of the blossoms God has made. God plans no less for us. Perhaps one day we will awaken to find that we can fly to feast on the beauty and love God has prepared for those who love Him.

Most humans are not eager to die, to find out exactly what happens in the afterlife. We want "heaven", whatever that means in each of our minds, but most of us prefer to delay that event as long as possible. Reminds one of the Joe Diffie song, *Prop Me Up Beside the Jukebox if I Die,* with the words "Lord I want to go to heaven, but I don't want to go tonight". We want to postpone that inevitable date with death if at all possible.

Wanting to live forever, right here on earth, a fringe element of the population believes that death is not inevitable. Some scientists are working toward the very goal of helping humans live for indefinite periods of time. In fact, according to Ray Kurzweil, the famous American futurist, our inventions have developed to the point where, by merging technology with the human body, we will soon be able to live indefinitely right here on earth. As early as 2005 Kurzweil was daily ingesting 250 supplements and taking a variety of other measures designed to enable him to live long enough for technology to take over, empowering him to live forever. He referred to the "exponential growth of information technology," predicting the use of computers the size of blood cells making their way through our bodies and connecting to the cloud. He says this is likely to occur by the year 2030. This leaves me speculating that instead of consulting a physician or surgeon to cure our ailments we may be visiting a computer repair shop to re-boot or re-program our bodies.

There could be interesting scenarios for our health care workers, requiring full-scale modifications to current health care systems. I'm not so sure a myriad of minicomputers coursing through my body would give me much confidence of life everlasting. Computers have been known to crash.

"Thanks, Ray, but no thanks," That's my response to Ray Kurzweil's ideas. "Earth is a great place for the healthy, the wealthy and the wise, but it has more than its share of problems, particularly for the poor, the lame and the diseased. I want to live forever, but there are much better places than this earth. I think God has a superior plan."

God's plan seems to be life, with its beauty, joy and pleasure, together with interludes of disease, disability and disasters until we reach our destination: death. We are not sure we like or buy into God's plan. The prevailing attitude is that life is God's greatest gift. Like Ray Kurzweil, most of us do everything we can to cling to it for as long as we can. And we largely ignore, despise or try to avoid God's gifts of disease, disability, disaster and death. Every human either personally experiences these gifts or has occasions to help fellow humans through these trials of our lives. Each of these greater gifts brings humankind closer together by giving us opportunities to mirror God's love, to practice sympathy and empathy as well as to engage in charitable works. We know that nothing on earth lasts forever: not life, nor pain, nor pleasure, nor sorrow. So, death, rather than life, is God's plan for receiving the greatest gift. It is the only pathway to heaven, to eternal life.

Jesus often talked about "the plan". But in describing God's plan, our ultimate goal of heaven, Jesus encourages us to think for ourselves. Rarely does he give concrete descriptions of the afterlife. Rather, he uses metaphors and similes, his parables, to describe what is unfathomable and indescribable to mere humans. He leaves room for us to imagine, dream and reach our own conclusions about the place called Heaven, his Father's home. Jesus' stories are easy and fun to remember. They give us a message. Yet there is almost always room for some interpretation. At various times he described heaven as a great banquet, a wedding feast, a mustard seed and leaven. He also mentioned that in his Father's house there are many rooms. Maybe there is one for us!

Many religious people believe only adherents to their specific beliefs have a reservation in one of those rooms in heaven. As I see it, we have two choices when we attempt to comprehend heaven. Either heaven is a tiny place, only for a select few, or it is a massive place which *could* hold much, or maybe all, of the universe. It depends on our view of God. Will He only accept worship and praise from those who follow a pre-ordained formula, or is He a welcoming, loving God who created diversity and loves all creation, wanting all of us to be with Him? The answer is obvious. *The real hard question is: do we want to be with God enough to follow The Golden Rule, to love God and love our neighbours? – all of them!*

So, what is heaven really like? In his book, *Proof of Heaven*, Dr. Eben Alexander, M.D. describes his near-death experiences with bird, angel, and butterfly-like creatures filling the universe with unimaginable beauty, colour, light, sound and love. He describes meeting a "guide" taking him on his novice flight into the afterlife, *"When first I saw her, we were riding along together on an intricately patterned surface, which after a moment I recognized as the wing of a butterfly. In fact, millions of butterflies were all around us—vast fluttering waves of them, dipping down into the woods and coming back up around us again. It was a river of life and colour, moving through the air."*

If we delve into holy books, we will get some clues about heaven. Those of us who are nearing the *afterlife* might consider what lies ahead. I was encouraged to do so this year. Going to church most Sundays, I listen to the sermons, mostly enjoying them, trying to glean a message. But I don't often remember sermons for very long - sometimes a few minutes, occasionally a few hours, a day or two at most. They go in one ear, out the other, rarely parking in my brain for any extended duration. However, one homily from a Sunday in 2018 stands out in my mind as an exception. Our parish priest, Father Phil, commenting on that Sunday's Gospel – the Kingdom of Heaven is like a mustard seed (Matthew 13:31) - asked us to make up our own comparisons, suggesting that we might like to envision what Heaven is like.

Let's follow the advice of Father Phil. Let's dream, speculate and imagine what awaits us as we journey into the afterlife. Some folks have difficulty believing there is an afterlife, or a Heaven, and that it is everlasting or infinite. I have no problem with it at all. In fact, I find it difficult to imagine otherwise. Can anything ever be infinite? Well, yes! Take our universe for example. Scientists tell us it doesn't end, and common sense tells us that you can't reach the end of our universe. You don't come to a brick wall or a fence with a big poster or flashing neon sign saying, "You have come to the edge of the universe. There is nothing on the other side of this barrier."

So, if our universe goes on, and on, and on, and on forever, is it possible that we might do the same?

And if we are to believe some of the teachings of Jesus, the afterlife can be filled with wonder and awe and marvels.

If so, what awaits us? I like to believe that what awaits us is very different for each of us. As humans, we have similarities, but we are created to be individuals. We all have our individual likes, dislikes, preferences and loves. Our opinions as to what is an ideal Heaven can be as varied as our preferences regarding an ideal temperature, the saltiness or spiciness of our food, our desire for solitude or companionship, our preference for comedy or tragedy, our love or abhorrence of jazz, blues, rock 'n roll, rap, easy listening, big band, country music or bluegrass. If God is truly a God of love, and I believe He is, Heaven will be big and open and loving enough to accommodate the quirks, preferences and desires of everyone worthy to enter and remain there.

Heaven will be something like a band playing a wondrous, beautiful, marvellous melody with each of us hearing only the genre and instruments and vocals and rhythm that appeal most to our senses, or if we just want peace and quiet, we might hear absolutely nothing. It will be something like eating in an unbelievable banquet hall where the menu is infinitely varied to appeal to everyone's taste buds. And the wine is exquisite. It all comes from the same limitless carafe, but it tastes amazing to everyone. We drink all we like, we are always happy, but we are never drunk or hungover. Or maybe it won't be like that at all for you. Maybe you don't care for music or fine food and wine. Maybe you like to eat in solitude and enjoy a big juicy loaded hamburger, with onion rings, fries and root beer without concerning yourself about the salt, fat, sugar and cholesterol content of what you are consuming. Do you think God can accommodate that? You can bet your big belly on that one.

What is Heaven for me? Well, I enjoy challenges. Maybe it's the realization that when I am challenged, I know that the result will not be perfection, but that success or achievement is all relative and that even if there is no perfection, maybe I can keep improving. I am finding that writing a book is like that. Relationships are often like that. Marriage is like that. Life is like that. And certainly, golf is like that. So, after the music and dancing and fine dining, is Heaven one big challenging golf course? I like to think so.

After death, when all the paperwork is completed and all my sins are deleted from the hard drive of the big computer in the sky, I am probably going golfing with all my favourite golfing buddies. And there are a few others who might like to join us, maybe Tiger Woods, Phil Mickelson and Annika Sorenstam or some of the veterans like Arnold, Sammy or Jack. It would be more than a foursome, but in Heaven that is allowed. We have all the time in the world, -er, I mean, in the universe. Some, or all these people might not want to golf, they might not want to golf with me, or they might have a different vision of Heaven and not want to golf at all. It doesn't matter. It's their heaven too. I imagine that Jesus will want to play a few rounds and that would be the thrill of a lifetime - er, a death time - for us. Whoever tees up will have an absolute blast.

In Heaven the beer cart ladies are real Angels, but the pin placement personnel are real Devils.... a little like on earth.

Maybe golf isn't your cup of tea. Lest Jesus hear mumbling and grumbling about my vision of Heaven from the non-golfers, remember that in my vision of Heaven each of us gets to create their own slice of Paradise.

But my speculations of what lies ahead tend to be selfish: what I want! Probably Heaven is much more inclusive, about giving and getting, about mutual healing of physical, spiritual and psychological wounds accumulated over a lifetime of human frailty. Heaven is about love and forgiveness. It is more about the prodigal son, or daughter, returning home to a loving and forgiving Father after a life of selfishness and greed.

Is it possible that what we call "the afterlife" will be no less a miracle than the miracle of life itself?

Chapter 27
Making Heaven/Creating Hell

"You don't go to heaven; you learn how to live in heaven now. And no one lives in heaven alone. Either you learn how to live in communion with the human race and with all that God has created, or, quite simply, you're not ready for heaven." - Fr. Richard Rohr, OFM

    A Buddhist proverb states: "To every man is given a key to the gates of heaven. The same key opens the gates of hell." Many of us tend to believe the religious traditions of "Heaven" and "Hell" as a place God will send us to for being good or being bad. Being raised Roman Catholic, I interpreted the afterlife in much the same way. Somewhere,

God draws a line in the sand; if we cross it, we are forever doomed - and God is to blame for creating us, allowing us to be sinners and then punishing us for it. I now see the world, life and the afterlife much differently. My belief is much more like the Buddhist proverb. God gave me the key. Which gate am I opening?

In His wisdom, God gave us body, mind and soul. We have almost no control of our bodies, except for our choices to exercise or not and to ingest healthful or harmful products. Otherwise nature takes its course: our bodies slowly deteriorate until we die, or they expire rapidly by disease or accident. Our minds are part of the body (the brain) and part of the soul (attitude, spirit). As the brain is part of the body, the physical, it too deteriorates. We have some limited control over the use our brain, but that control is fleeting.

Now we come to the soul, our attitudes of love or hate, sharing or selfishness, suspicion and discrimination or inclusiveness and friendship. I have no choice about the fate of my body, little choice of the fate of my mind, but complete choice over the fate of my spirit (my soul). If I believe our God is a God of love, of sharing, of peace and of truth, I know what choices I must make, even though they may at times appear difficult. Therein, I make my own heaven. Or I can choose to exclude, to discriminate against anyone or anything I label as different, not worthy of my love and respect: a person of different colour, a different religion, a different aptitude or a different physical appearance, and thereby I can create my own hell. Humans have done so in the past; we continue to create hell for ourselves and much of God's creation. Richard Rohr's meditation from Thursday, March 30, 2017 entitled *God's Fingerprints*, tells us as much, "*It is hard to imagine how different the last 800 years might have been if this truly catholic vision had formed more Christians. But our common seeing has been partial, punitive, and prejudicial. The individual was allowed to decide and discriminate as to where and if God's image would be recognized and honoured. Sinners, heretics, witches, Muslims, slaves, Jews, blacks, natives, buffalo, whales, elephants, land, and water were all the losers. And we dared to call ourselves monotheists or believers in one coherent world.*" Oh, I can make all kinds of reasons or excuses about why "they" don't deserve my love, my friendship, my support, but the decision is completely my own.

Heaven and hell are what we make them. If we believe that God loves all His creation, and we want to be where God is - in the place we call Heaven - maybe we, too, are challenged to love and preserve all God's creation, not just those people and objects which appeal most to us. Perhaps universal acceptance and practice of the *Golden Rule* will eventually result in Heaven on earth. If God truly loves all His creation and He has given us free will, is it possible that the only real Hell is the one we create for ourselves through our words and our actions, particularly the marginalizing of those who are most vulnerable?

Humans have difficulty imagining that they will become amazing, loving spirits, or saints. But with vision and action, we can make it happen. God has ordained that, through Nature, our physical bodies and our brains will change. But He has given us free will; so, He will not change our souls, our attitudes, and our spirit. Only we can do that, and whatever we choose in life is likely what we choose in death. Do we really create our own Heaven? Do we really make our own Hell?

Let us create wisely!

Gerald M. Sliva

Chapter 28
Packing My Bags

"Life does not cease to be funny when people die any more than it ceases to be serious when people laugh." - George Bernard Shaw

    This chapter is written for folks who are dying. News flash: we are all dying, just at varying velocities.
    Most of us have considered our departures from this life, and what happens to our being (our body and our soul) after we die, but the vast majority of us have not discussed this with our friends and loved ones. Serious considerations about death rank along with other topics too sensitive to discuss: religion, sex and politics. Somehow, we seem to be under the illusion that if avoid talking about death, we can prevent it from happening. Or, maybe we believe our loved ones want to avoid the topic too. Besides, I'm too busy living to waste my time with planning my dying. I really don't want to pack my bags for that journey just yet. Furthermore, I haven't used up my hoard of sale priced

coffee and dental floss. It is said that we are guaranteed nothing in life but death and taxes. Taxes have arrived. Death will too.

Death is our final prayer. Prayer and death are really surrendering – I don't mean giving up – I mean wholehearted acceptance of Eternity and the Supreme Being who gave us life and who will give us our New Life. It is the final act in what we humans call free will. I really have two choices: bitterness because my life is ending or gratitude for the gift of life I was given. I will try to say a heartfelt, grateful good-bye.

In 2018 I attended the funeral and was pallbearer for a person I never knew. He was a member of the Knights of Columbus, and because he died leaving no known living relatives, the parish priest requested that the local Knights attend and be pallbearers. The cohort was small. There was no eulogy. We sang a couple hymns. The homily was very brief. The Mass and service were direct, plain and without fanfare. In other words, "Beautiful"!

I have attended funerals which left me less than impressed. Some have been so long, with the eulogy so detailed as to have possibly been published as a memoir. Perhaps that would have been better. Then we would have had a choice: read it, or not. I know and understand the need for eulogies, remembering, mourning, grieving and sorrowing. This is especially important for close relatives and intimate friends. I also know that often when a church is filled with people, most want to say their goodbyes, express their sympathies and get on with their own lives. Maybe I and my circle of aging friends are far too critical, but after some funerals we have often discussed the lengthy nature of some eulogies, with numerous relatives and friends eulogizing far more than appropriate. When one sits through close to two hours of funeral, the spirit is willing, but the rear end is sore, and the attention is minimal.

I have wondered about what sort of farewell I might wish my relatives and friends to experience when my own life ends. Contemplating my own eventual demise, I thought it best to officially reveal to my survivors my views of an appropriate send-off. It is said, "We all gotta go". Yes, we do! But just because I have died, is no reason for mere acquaintances to suffer the agony of a long, boring funeral service. If my closest surviving relatives feel the need to support each other, to mourn and to grieve, I urge them to do so in smaller, more intimate gatherings. I've heard a few wise priests say that funerals are for the living, not for the dead; so, my survivors will have the last word on this. But, if you will humour me, while I'm still here I will state my idea of a good funeral:

- Cremation
- I am Catholic, and would like a short, simple Mass at my departure.
- A brief eulogy as well as an abbreviated homily. (I suggest no more than ten minutes for each.)
- Three or four inspirational hymns with a vocal range suitable for the singing voice of an average individual. Some suggestions: How Great Thou Art, Amazing Grace, Make Me a Channel of Your Peace, Lord of the Dance.
- A joyful gathering after the service. Lots to eat. An optional glass of wine for each attendee.

Pondering My Departure:

This is a lifetime of good-byes. Eventually I must say good-bye to life itself. How can I say a good "good-bye"?

As a last gift to my survivors, do I want to leave them some suggestions regarding my funeral? If I do, there is no time like the present. Death comes suddenly!

Do my survivors know if I prefer cremation or traditional burial? Does it matter to me, or to them?

Have I prepared a will? How can my Last Will and Testament be a joyful expression of *The Golden Rule*?

How can my final surrender, my acceptance of death, knowing that I really control *nothing* in this world and that my loving Creator is in charge, be my most fervent prayer?

Do I want to share this chapter with my loved ones to start a discussion on this sensitive topic?

Do I want to hide or burn this book so that no one raises the topics of religion, sex, politics and, most particularly, death?

"According to most studies, people's number one fear is public speaking. Number two is death. Death is number two!? Does that sound right? That means to the average person, if you go to a funeral, you're better off in the casket than doing the eulogy." – Jerry Seinfeld

Gerald M. Sliva

Epilogue

"The unexamined life is not worth living" - Socrates

I have described, referred to, and examined some of my own experiences with religion, sex and politics. By doing this, my wish is that my readers were encouraged to do the same. Having some issues with Roman Catholicism, as well as with other religions, I was encouraged to ask many questions about the meaning of life.

In my research for the writing of this book, I read several articles and books about a variety of religions, many proclaiming to have all the answers to the meaning of life. Through this study, I learned that many holy books and most religions have value and clues to the meaning of life. But I have also learned that throughout history some people have interpreted their scriptures simply to justify racism, greed, lust for power and a plethora of other evils.

I had two objectives in writing this book:
- To encourage inquiry, to seek truth, both for myself and for my readers. I tried to do that by

using thought-provoking quotations and probing questions.
- My second objective was to raise money for worthy charities.

Two charities which I support are Siloam Mission, which I mentioned in chapter 20, and the Sierra Leone Action Mission (SLAM) which is building a high school for orphans in Koidu, Sierra Leone.

Siloam Mission provides meals, shelter, clothing and counselling for the homeless in Winnipeg, Manitoba. SLAM operates an orphanage in Koidu, Sierra Leone, which has been decimated by war and Ebola, where there are few books, few libraries and few schools. Most of the population lives on about one dollar a day. A good education will help Sierra Leoneans think and act in ways which will enable them to help themselves and their fellow citizens.

By purchasing this book, you have helped me to reach my second objective. On behalf of the orphans of Sierra Leone and the homeless in Winnipeg, thank you so much! One hundred percent of royalties from the sale of this book will go to these and other worthy charities.

Whether or not I have fully reached my first objective depends on each of us. As individuals, we may not have discovered the meaning of life, but perhaps we have walked together, seeking truth. May you be blessed in your search and in all your good works!

Do I agree with Socrates? Is the unexamined life not worth living?

The End.

Or is it really the beginning?

Meditation, Reflection, Discussion

By now the reader knows that this is a book of questions rather than answers. As I concluded each chapter, I realized that there were even more questions left unanswered. Here they are for pondering, discussion, meditation or even action.

Chapter 1 - Something to think about:

Research has shown that many people blindly accept information from their religious affiliation or their political party. And they automatically reject information from other religions or political parties. Do I critically analyze information prior to making judgments?

How can blind faith hurt a religious or political cause?

The Bible events, in many instances, relate stories of people receiving messages from God. Do I believe people receive direct messages from Jesus or God?

Chapter 2 - Examining my motivation:

Do I hang on to my beliefs because they are authentic, or because I am too lazy or too fearful to assess them critically?

What made me pick up this book? Was it the cover, *The Golden Rule*, or the topics of religion, sex and politics?

Am I afraid to critically examine my faith, what I really believe? Or is uncertainty an aid to true exploration?

Chapter 3 - More Questions:

If I were born and raised under completely different circumstances, I would have different faith and beliefs. Would I be wrong in what I believed?

Is it possible that I am biased or prejudiced for or against people of any culture, race, religion, politics or sexual orientation? Can I identify specific interactions or experiences which may have contributed to these feelings or biases?

"I yam what I yam, and that's all what I yam". If the conditions of my birth are an accident, my uncontrollable heredity, what can I do to improve my lot? What can society do to mitigate my condition?

If I have been blessed with the treasures of wisdom, gold, health, or physical and mental strength, do I have increased moral and ethical responsibilities? Does the Golden Rule affect my interpersonal and interracial behaviour?

Difficult questions! Where are the answers?

Jesus gave us one answer. What is my opinion of it? *"When a man has had a great deal given him, a great deal will be demanded of him; when a man has had a great deal given him on trust, even more will be expected of him."*- Luke 12:48

Chapter 4 - Points to Ponder:

How did my own religious and spiritual formative years influence my view of God and religion?

Do I know anything about religions other than my own? Do I want to? If yes, what could I gain? If not, what am I afraid of losing?

Chapter 5 - Further Reflection:

Should there be stricter penalties for hazing and bullying?

What can *The Golden Rule* teach us about initiation rites as well as the application of appropriate discipline in abusive situations?

Do I believe sexually segregated boarding schools are satisfactory training grounds for appropriate social interaction?

Chapter 6 - Food For Thought:

Where did I receive my initial misinformation or information about sexual matters? What information did I provide to my offspring? Was it adequate and appropriate?

Do parents generally do a good job of providing accurate and appropriate information about sex? If not, how could parents receive the guidance they need to do better?

How can parents, educators and religious use the Golden Rule to illustrate relevant information about sexual conduct?

If children shouldn't learn about sex in "the gutter" or on the internet, where is the best place for them to learn about it?

Chapter 7 - Reflecting Further:

Are there political solutions to humanity's problems?

In domestic politics and international conflicts, each faction believes that God is on their side. Delusion? Is it more likely that God is on the side of peace, good will and love?

Do our political and religious divisions prevent us from arriving at solutions to society's problems?

Have Western democracy's divisive politics and religion created irreconcilable differences together with a revulsion for and mistrust of politics and spirituality? How can these be overcome?

How does *The Golden Rule* apply to countries and governments as well as to individuals?

Would the adoption of *The Golden Rule* as a guiding principle of the United Nations be a step in the right direction?

Chapter 8 - Things to Consider:

Has humanity turned politics into its religion and religion into its god?

Separation of church and state? Is it possible?

Are political leaders' emphasis in winning re-election and their focus on party platforms rather than a focus on

The Golden Rule and the needs of their constituents preventing our democracies from achieving excellence?

Will all democracies and religions implode or commit suicide unless they adopt *The Golden Rule?*

Chapter 9 - Further Consideration:

Do I believe the theory of evolution is compatible with the belief in creation?

If the theory of evolution is being taught in our schools, should it be presented in conjunction with the belief in creationism? Are we afraid to consider both possibilities? Why?

Chapter 10 - Consider This:

What have I created out of love?
Of which of my creations am I particularly fond? Why?
For me, what is the most beautiful object in all of nature?
What am I doing to preserve the treasures of nature? Or am I wasteful, a litterer and a thoughtless polluter, leaving creation in a mess for future generations to clean up?

How can I apply *The Golden Rule* in my everyday interactions with animals, plants and the environment as well as with fellow humans?

Chapter 11 - Questions of Faith and Reasoning:

What is my own understanding, belief, scepticism or faith in the words of the Bible?

How much does the disciples' dying for their beliefs help my belief?

Do I believe the Bible literally? Or do I accept some of the Bible stories as metaphorical? The Old Testament of the Bible is over 2000 years old. The New Testament is about 2000 years old. What is its primary message for everyday life in modern society? Is it relevant to me today?

Is the Bible intended to be read in its entirety, or is it more a road map or GPS (God Positioning System) which we ought to turn to when we lose our way, or when we simply want to find a better path than our current one?

Chapter 12 - Questions for consideration:

Do I believe there is intelligent life elsewhere in the universe? For that matter, do I believe there is intelligent life here on earth?

If space aliens come to our planet, is there any chance we would treat them any better than we treat anyone else who is different from us?

If human-like aliens exist on other planets, is it likely they would have religions? Would they have a Golden Rule equivalent?

How would I react if I encountered an intelligent being which (who?) was different from my image of human?

Chapter 13 - Further reflection:

Do I have any real faith at all, or am I filled with doubt?

If I am an atheist, what convinces me that atheism is the truth?

Am I a believer? If not, what would it take to make me one?

Is it necessary to have unshakeable faith in order to reach the place we call heaven? Does God exclude those who have not heard of God or who do not believe in God? Or do I believe God has a special place for all people of good will, whether or not they are believers?

Chapter 14 - Something to Consider:

If the whole world proclaims *The Golden Rule* as its mantra, how do I reconcile the pervasiveness of greed, jealousy, hate and murder in all societies?

What does *The Golden Rule* mean to me in my daily life?

Chapter 15 - Questions for Consideration:

What is more important: religion or spirituality? Prayer or charitable works?

Deepak Chopra says, *"Religion is belief in someone else's experience. Spirituality is having your own experience."* Do I agree with Deepak?

Is it too easy to start a new religion?

If a group does not ascribe to *The Golden Rule*, should it be permitted the tax breaks afforded religions?

The Bible states that Jesus prayed *"May they all be one. Father, may they be one in us, as you are in me and I am in you, so that the world may believe it was you who sent me."* (John 17:21) Are church leaders' emphasis on differences in dogma and ritual rather than focusing on our similar beliefs and *The Golden Rule* preventing us from achieving Jesus' vision?

Chapter 16 - Points to ponder:

Is church attendance important in developing a realistic image of my goals and purpose in life?

How do the flaws in church leaders affect my faith, my worship, my church attendance, my financial support of religion?

How does my church attendance or avoidance facilitate the implementation of *The Golden Rule*?

Chapter 17 - Something to think about:

Do I focus too much on what I *believe* are the sins of others?

If my son, daughter, grandson or granddaughter "came out" with non-traditional sexuality would I accept and love them? *Really?* How about my spouse? Everyone who is LGBTQ is someone's offspring. How do I react to them?

If I were green, or black, or mentally or physically disabled, or transsexual, or gay, how would I want to be treated?

How does *The Golden Rule* apply in the treatment of anyone whom I regard as *different*?

Chapter 18 - Further thoughts, actions and stirring the pot:

What are my views on mandatory celibacy for Catholic clergy? Perhaps I might re-read and ponder Father Richard Rohr's statement in Chapter 18 of this book.

Does mandatory celibacy cause many potentially excellent candidates to screen themselves out of the priesthood?

Does writing letters to any hierarchy have any measurable impact? Do I waste my time writing a letter to the Pope or any other person in power? Bishop Robert Barron, in his August 30, 2018 reflection thinks not. He says, "How do I fight? Look: You fight by writing a letter to your Bishop, a letter to the Pope. You fight by keeping people's feet to the fire."

Would open discussions on sexuality reduce the shame, guilt and crimes?

Married, female, or gay clergy would create a whole new set of issues. What are my opinions?

How does this whole chapter reflect the application, acceptance or rejection of *The Golden Rule*?

Chapter 19 - Mindful Meditation:

Forgiveness does not mean tolerating or enabling physical, emotional, psychological or sexual abuse of any kind at home, in the workplace, in any personal relationship or in the whole of society. If I suffer from abuse should I seek professional counselling?

Have I done all I can to forgive others? To forgive myself?

When I pray the Lord's Prayer, do I mean what I say? Is my heart in my prayer?

How is *The Golden Rule* reflected in The Lord's Prayer?

What am I doing to work as well as pray for God's kingdom to come?

Chapter 20 - Action and Contemplation:

Does charitable giving create dependency?

If I believe in charity, where should I focus my efforts? Why?

What is more important: charitable monetary giving or charitable works?

What is my reaction and what thoughts go through my mind when I see a beggar on the streets? Do I avoid the person, or do I actively seek to determine their needs? What is the best course of action?

If prayer is surrender to a Higher Power, how are charitable works some of the most powerful prayers?

How can charity be one of the most valid expressions of *The Golden Rule*?

Do I have a story of neighbourly charity that I want to share? Please send it to **myconundra@gmail.com**

Chapter 21 - Food for Thought:

Does Jesus want us to be Christians? Or does he hang his holy head in sorrow that we try to pretend that we are in his camp, but do little to demonstrate our allegiance to his teachings?

Am I a little peeved with Jesus for giving me a seemingly impossible task? Am I disappointed in my own reaction? Or do I try harder?

Is true love synonymous with *The Golden Rule*?

What is the real antithesis of love? Is it hate? Fear? Aloofness? Suspicion? Something else?

Is true love an unrealistic goal, making Jesus a dreamer?

Chapter 22 - More prayer:

Prayer is personal. What is my most heartfelt prayer?

Do I recognize and appreciate the daily miracles in my life?

When I express gratitude to *anyone*, how am I demonstrating *The Golden Rule*?

Chapter 23 - Remembering Tears:

What was my most precious shedding of tears? Was it a spiritual time? Shall I take a moment to thank my Creator for that experience?

Do I believe sharing tears of joy or sorrow with someone I love will help to strengthen my relationship and deepen my love?

How does the sharing of emotions strengthen the application of *The Golden Rule* in my everyday life?

How can the release of tears be genuine prayer?

Chapter 24 – Further reflection or action:

Do I believe that there are connections and contacts between the physical world and the spirit world?

Do I believe Jesus' resurrection vividly demonstrates the links between the physical and spiritual? Cynthia Bourgeault, Episcopal priest and mystic certainly does. She says, "What Jesus so profoundly demonstrates to us in his passage from death to life is that the walls between the realms are paper thin. Along the entire ray of creation, the "mansions" are interpenetrating and mutually permeable by love. The death of our physical form is not the death of our individual personhood."

Chapter 25 – Knowing:

If I focus on each person's inner beauty, am I living the *Golden Rule*?

How can I demonstrate that I believe there is much more to each person than their "Earth suit"?

Chapter 26 – Questions for consideration:

What is my image of an ideal heaven? Or do I even believe in heaven?

What do I think I will be doing after I die? Will I be sitting on a cloud playing a harp, or will I be doing something more inspirational and adventurous? Or will my existence and being simply disappear?

For the non-spiritual, non-believing folks among us, the laws of thermodynamics state that energy can neither be created nor destroyed. Einstein proved that energy and matter are really two states of the same existence. Does that mean that even when our body dies, our energy *("soul")* lives on?

If bacon and chocolate are the health foods in heaven, will broccoli and liver be the confections in hell?

Chapter 27 - Something to Consider:

Do I really create my own reality? How?

What can I do to create heaven right here on earth?

Could universal acceptance and practice of *The Golden Rule* result in Heaven on earth?

If I believe God truly loves all His creation and He has given us free will, is it possible that the only real Hell is the one we create ourselves through our words and our actions, particularly the marginalizing of those who are most vulnerable?

Chapter 28 - Pondering My Departure:

Last chance to share this chapter or to burn the book! Your choice!

Do I want to share this chapter, or maybe the whole book, with my loved ones to start a discussion on these sensitive topics?

Do I want to contemplate this issue more fully? Richard Rohr's meditation from April 3, 2019 might be of interest: https://cac.org/living-fully-2019-04-03/

Do I want to hide or burn this book so that no one raises the topics of religion, sex, politics and, most particularly, death?

Acknowledgements

Writing and authorship is a solitary task, but it is never concluded in isolation. Many good people have supported my publishing adventure which began with the publication of *Barking From the Front Porch* and continues with my *Conundra* experiment.

First, thank you to the love of my life, my wife of 55 years, Cecilia, who patiently reads my musings and tells me exactly what she thinks. In like manner, our son, Greg, always provides incisive big-picture feedback. Without Cecilia and Greg, none of my writing would be published.

A good editor is worth her weight in gold. I hesitate to ask my sister, Barbara what she weighs. Besides, I can't afford to pay her in gold. But her honest and constructive commentary have helped me to rethink and revise my narrative, improve my structure and reduce/eliminate grammatical errors. Barbara is treasure to any writer. Further, as Barbara was editing, she shared my manuscript with her husband, Dr. Bruce Berscheid who has provided insightful and valuable commentary on the content of this book. Thank you so much, Barbara and Bruce!

Controversial topics like religion demand an extra level of content editing. Many thanks to my good friends Don and Joyce Nakrieko as well as Maumer Hazirovic who provided constructive and helpful commentary on the content of this book. You are valued friends!

Two individuals who have been the source of so much inspiration to me in my writing, at first glance might seem like polar opposites: Richard Rohr, Roman Catholic priest and David Meakes, agnostic humanitarian. After I introduced David to Father Richard's meditations, David and I frequently discussed the meditation themes, with David often commenting that he and Father Richard had similar ideas and promoted similar values. I am forever indebted to them both for unintentionally spurring me to consider and to author reflections on some of what I regard to be the important things in life. Thank you, my friends!

(Note: It is with sadness that I report that my friend David Meakes passed away on July 1, 2019 as I was penning this manuscript.)

To have value, a book must be read. To be read, it must be distributed, marketed, sold. All my friends and relatives have bought and promoted my *Barking*. But I would be remiss in not identifying super-marketers, my sister and brother-in-law, Marg and Steve Suik. They own Wadena Bakery, and together with their amazing Boston Creams and other delicious products, they have sold numerous quantities of my *Barking From the Front Porch*. Thank you, Steve and Margaret, for your valued support.

To detail all the ways in which friends and relatives have humoured me in my publishing adventure, I would have to write another whole book. I won't do that here, but I want to recognize some wonderful and very special people who have helped me along the way.

My relatives: Greg, Grace and Robyn Sliva; Don Sliva; Barbara (my editor) and Bruce Berscheid; Jim and Shannon Sliva; Steve and Marg Suik (super-bakers); John and Darlene Sliva; Terry and Wanda Slobodian; Larry and Rita Novakowski; Father Rudolph Nowakowski; Mike and Iris Nowakowski; Donna Frandsen.

My friends: Don and Joyce Nakrieko; David Meakes; George and Morris Kulyk; Gayle Morrow; Eric and Flo Lindgren; Bill Sowa.

My many American friends and supporters from Desert Skies RV Park and Quail Run RV Park in Arizona.

My friends and former co-workers: Mary Lou Deck and Sharon Halford as well my many other friends and supporters from the Human Resources Canada offices.

My friends, coffee and golf buddies and idea people: Marcel, Moe, Brian, T. Don, Klem, Ed and Bob. There is a song by Randy Travis called *Forever and Ever, Amen*. One line in that song goes: *"As long as old men sit and talk about the weather."* News alert: The old men I know and with whom I associate talk about topics more interesting than the weather. They talk about the issues I have raised in this book: religion, politics, sex and death.

Thank you also to the many people who left reviews of my *Barking* on the Amazon website. Reviews tend to be the lifeblood of authors. More reviews equate to more interest in the subject matter, and more sales.

In concluding my acknowledgements, I give special thanks to Gerd Altmann and Pixabay for providing a wonderful selection of photos, one of which I have used as my book cover image.

Big hugs and thanks to everyone who has supported me in any way.

Finally, thank **you** for buying and reading *Conundra, The Golden Rule Revisited*. You have supported some of my favourite charities. 100% of the royalties from the sale of this book go to support a school being built for the poorest of the poor in Sierra Leone, the homeless in Winnipeg, Manitoba and other worthwhile charities.

Bibliography, Reference and Reading List

Knowing the Doctrines of the Bible, Myer Pearlman, Gospel Publishing House

Understanding the Bible, Stephen L. Harris, Mayfield Publishing Company

The Four Gospels, L. Thomas Holdcroft, CeeTeC Publishing

Daily Dose of Knowledge: Brilliant Thoughts, West Side Publishing

More Than a Carpenter, Josh McDowell/Sean McDowell, Tyndale House Publishers Inc.

Religion Can Make Sense, Clint Lee Scott, Universalist Publishing House, Boston Massachusetts

Christian Mystics, Matthew Fox, New World Library

Mother Teresa, The Authorized Biography, Navin Chawla, Element Books Inc.

The Greatest Thing in the World, Henry Drummond, Thomas Y. Crowell Company

How Came the Bible, Edgar J. Goodspeed, Pillar Books

Proof of Heaven, Eben Alexander, M.D., Simon and Schuster Paperbacks

Albert Schweitzer, A Study of His Philosophy of Life, Gabriel Langfeldt, George Allen & Unwin Ltd.

The Light Within Us, Albert Schweitzer, The Philosophical Library, Inc

The Jerusalem Bible, Reader's Edition, Doubleday and Company, Inc., Garden City, New York

Reader's Digest, April 2014, "How We Pray" by Lise Funderburg

Gandhi, His Life and Message for the World by Louis Fischer, The New American Library

Why We Can't Wait, Martin Luther King, Jr., Signet Classics

Dream, The Words and Inspiration of Martin Luther King, Jr., Blue Mountain Press, Boulder, Colorado

The Story of My Experiments with Truth, Mohandas K. Gandhi, Autobiography, Dover Publications, Inc, New York

Perspective, The Golden Rule, David Meakes, Litfire Publishing

Richard Rohr's Daily Meditations at **cac.org**

www.Brainyquote.com
www.wisdomquotes.com
www.goodreads.com

More by this author.

Gerald Sliva has also written the popular book *Barking From the Front Porch*, a humorous, heart-warming, nostalgic memoir of growing up in a small town hotel.

In Praise of Barking From the Front Porch:

"After reading your "Hair Raising Experience" I laughed so hard I almost peed myself .... truly a comedic experience...." - Ed, Manitoba, Canada

"*Barking From the Front Porch* is an enchanting, side-splitting, heartfelt life story that has taken this reader into the author's world where life was "perfectly" simple. This is a book that should be in every family's library!" - Wanda, Ontario, Canada

"I am loving reading your book!" – Jean, California, USA

"I just received the book today and read it this afternoon, with tears and laughter." – Nadine, Alberta, Canada

"A great story Gerald, and I read it in two sittings. Brought back lots of memories and certainly shared a lot of similarities to our life growing up on the farm. Had me laughing till I cried and shedding a true tear in other parts. Thanks for sharing." - Morris, Alberta, Canada

"Gerry, I just finished your book and wanted to tell you how much I enjoyed it! You are a very wise and talented man. Loved the book! Keep writing. Look forward to book #2." – Barb, Alberta, Canada

Conclusion and Invitation

100% of the royalties from the sales of this book go to charity. I invite you to contribute further to two of the charities supported through the sales of this book. Here are their websites:
https://accountabledevelopment.org/
https://www.siloam.ca/
Accountable Development Works is the umbrella organization housing four worthy projects, one of which is the Sierra Leone orphanage and school build project.
Occasionally, I will update my followers about these charities, particularly the building of a school in Sierra Leone.
Please like and follow my Facebook page for updates and information on new books I may publish:
https://www.facebook.com/geraldmsliva/

Thank you again for you support.

Made in the USA
Columbia, SC
18 February 2020